Praise for

Intentional

Leadership

"Jane Kise has the ability to take the minutiae and complexity of leadership psychology and boil it down to the simple and the profound. She offers practical how-to recommendations that help intentional leaders achieve their intended results. Become the leader you want to be—intentionally."

> —**Robert Grede**, Best-Selling Author of *Naked Marketing: The Bare Essentials*; President, The Grede Company

"Jane Kise has done what other books on leadership have failed to do. She successfully takes us on a journey of understanding our natural leadership preferences and styles in a way that not only provides the 'Eureka!' moment, but compels us to apply the information in our daily lives and relationships. Kise's keen insights provide a refreshing, practical, and realistic approach to what it means to become a more effective leader. I will be using this book with leaders throughout our organization and in my own leadership development efforts."

> —**Roger Jansen**, Senior Vice President/CHRO, Spectrum Health System

"If you aspire to have the corner office or up your game, you need *Intentional Leadership*. Jane Kise shows leaders how to use intention and their innate personalities to improve results."

> —**Nordahl L. Brue**, Founder, Bruegger's Bagels

"Jane Kise has produced a book filled with practical suggestions and examples of leading with intentionality. Readers are forced to consider, 'Am I leading for career success, or am I leading as a calling?' while exploring their true leadership potential."

> —**Richard Bents**, President, Future Systems Consulting

"A comprehensive resource for all leaders who wish to gain a deeper understanding of their leadership strengths and potential blind spots. With its opportunities for personal reflection and action planning, this book will be an ongoing point of reference for leaders."

> —**Janelle Wills**, Director of Teaching and Learning,
> Independent Schools Queensland, Australia

Intentional
Leadership

Intentional
Leadership

12 LENSES
for Focusing Strengths, Managing Weaknesses,
and Achieving Your Purpose

Jane A. G. Kise

ALLWORTH PRESS
NEW YORK

Allworth Press books may be purchased in bulk at special discounts for sales promotion, corporate gifts, fund-raising, or educational purposes. Special editions can also be created to specifications. For details, contact the Special Sales Department, Allworth Press, 307 West 36th Street, 11th Floor, New York, NY 10018 or info@skyhorsepublishing.com.

15 14 13 12 11   5 4 3 2

Published by Allworth Press, an imprint of Skyhorse Publishing, Inc.
307 West 36th Street, 11th Floor, New York, NY 10018.

Allworth Press® is a registered trademark of Skyhorse Publishing, Inc.®, a Delaware corporation.

www.allworth.com

Cover and interior design by Rian Anderson
Library of Congress Cataloging-in-Publication Data is available on file.

ISBN: 978-1-62153-426-6
Ebook ISBN: 978-1-62153-419-8

Printed in the United States of America

For Linda Gilligan, who, besides being
a kindred spirit and dear friend, models
intentional leadership in all she does.

Acknowledgments

I couldn't very well write in isolation a book about valuing different strengths, perspectives, and priorities. From start to finish, my colleagues from the Association for Psychological Type International willingly joined me in discussing leadership dilemmas, their own experiences, and insights on managing the tensions inherent in leadership.

I would especially like to thank Richard Olson of Olson Consulting Group for the incredible amount of time he gave to helping me formulate my thoughts as well as invaluable critiques on several chapters. Sue Blair of Personality Dynamics, Ltd., sorted cards, gave advice on making the book more practical, and provided excellent revision suggestions on many of the chapters. Similarly, Sidney Craig Courtice generously commented on several revisions of the book's framework. Jim Dogan, Hile Rutledge, and Bob McAlpine also gave priceless early feedback.

Thank you to the members of the New Zealand Association for Psychological Type who joined in an early discussion of the key Lenses for Leadership. Thanks also to Clare and Barry Ayers, Paula and Martin Herring, Sandra Krebs Hirsh, Ann Holm, Kaki McCarthy, and Jason Whetstone, who were enthusiastic guinea pigs for finalizing the leadership priorities. All of you are great leadership models for making constructive use of differences.

Table of Contents

Intentional
Leadership

CHAPTER 1

Learning From Intentional—and Unintentional—Leaders

I intend to be a good leader. That statement is true for you, right? After all, I've never coached anyone who *intended* to be the inspiration for a "How to Work for a Jerk" workshop or a situation comedy.

There's a vast difference, though, between having good intentions and being an intentional leader. The intentional leaders I work with plan *how* they will lead, not just what they will accomplish as leaders.

Phone calls launch the majority of my work as a management consultant. Calls from intentional leaders go something like this:

> Hi, Jane. You worked with my team [or a colleague's team] at XYZ Company. I'm leading a new effort and want to start out on the right foot. Can you work with us so I can gain a clear picture of the ways my leadership style meshes with the strengths of my group and what areas or concerns I could easily overlook?

Intentional leaders have deep self-knowledge and recognize that their strengths come with blind spots. They know that every situation draws on their talents in ways that bring out inevitable limitations. They're intentional about identifying any potential problems as best they can.

Other calls follow this pattern:

Is this Jane? I doubt you can help me, but I got your name from _____.
The only thing the team I'm leading agrees on is that they hate me. They need
to learn how to resolve conflict and work together.

These leaders, too, have good intentions, and great strengths and skills. The vast majority has a clear picture of their business goals and how to accomplish them. But they aren't intentional about how they are going to lead, nor have they reflected on the impact of their leadership style, the good and the not-so-good. They don't ask questions like:

- Who will I be leading?
- What will motivate these particular individuals to reach our business or organizational goals?
- What defines our environment?
- What emphases and actions on my part will have the greatest positive impact on my team's performance?
- Where might my style fall short of what is needed in this situation?

In *The Truth About Leadership*, James Kouzes and Barry Posner summarize their decades-long study of high-performing leaders, emphasizing that people are most influenced by their most immediate manager. They caution leaders to internalize, "It is not a question of 'Will I make a difference?' Rather, it's 'What difference will I make?'"[1] At every level, it is what leaders actually do each day that determines whether employees think highly of their workplace, view the work as important, believe that integrity on the job matters, and feel motivated to put forth their best effort.

What do those who report to you see you doing each day? Do they see you creating? Learning? Interacting? Listening? Observing? Have you thought about how your actions influence your team members' vision and their connection to your organization?

The first step toward intentional leadership is carefully defining your priorities to convey what you mean to convey—what you'll emphasize in a particular situation. Is accountability one of your core priorities? Do you believe that collaboration or empowerment is essential to success?

Once you've identified your leadership priorities, the second step in becoming an intentional leader is to align your leadership actions to convey the importance that you attach to those priorities. If accountability is one of your priorities, then convey the importance of being accountable by modeling it. If collaboration or expertise or mentoring is a priority, then collaborate, be open about adding to your expertise, and find a mentee.

Step 1: Identify Your Leadership Priorities

Following are forty leadership priorities. (They also appear in the appendix on page 151.) Your task is to choose your top ten. Think about a specific leadership position, either your current role or one to which you aspire. As you read each priority, ask yourself, "To be successful as a leader in this role, do I need to model this priority?" Cross out any priorities to which you answer, "No, modeling this isn't essential in this particular situation." Then concentrate on the remaining priorities. Which are most essential? Remember, your list should include no more than ten.

1. **Accountability**: I establish realistic expectations and responsibility for outcomes, striving for clarity regarding what is and isn't under our control.

2. **Achievement**: I believe in setting worthy goals, planning for how to reach them, and then doing so.

3. **Adaptability**: I model being able to adjust to ever-changing circumstances, responding to the needs of the moment.

4. **Appreciation**: I want to create an atmosphere where people demonstrate respect for each other, regardless of expertise.

5. **Autonomy**: I foster teams in which each member can be effective when thinking and acting independently.

6. **Balance**: I want to model limits on work so that I and those with whom I work make time for family, health, leisure pursuits, nature, and relationships.

7. **Challenge**: I'm motivated by exciting problems or difficult, risk-filled tasks that enhance skills and prove competency.

8. **Collaboration**: I want to foster meaningful teamwork where people enjoy working together and keep everyone's best interests in mind.

9. **Connecting**: I believe that listening to understand the viewpoints, feelings, and aspirations of those I lead increases my effectiveness.

10. **Creativity with the known**: I value using sound judgment, proven routines, and known information for continuous improvement in practical matters.

11. **Creativity with the new**: I value using my imagination and inspirations to devise original ideas, theories, tools, methods, or plans that bring about change.

12. **Depth**: I want to be in charge of long-term, significant projects for which we pursue a major goal or develop important expertise.

13. **Dependability**: I want to be known as trustworthy and reliable, carrying out the charges I have been given.

14. **Discovery**: I explore choices, options, resources, learning opportunities, networks, friendships, theories, ideas, and so on; searching energizes me.

15. **Efficiency**: I want to organize our work environments, processes, tasks, and such, so that goals are met with little waste of time, talent, or materials.

16. **Empathy**: My style emphasizes stepping into the shoes of others and understanding their experiences, values, and points of view.

17. **Empowering**: I strive to enable others to learn to lead themselves and take the initiative in their work.

18. **Enjoyment**: I want to create a work environment that is inspiring, congenial, and playful, where people can find a touch of fun and humor.

19. **Experience**: I thrive when using our knowledge and past work, which are key to improving performance or to planning and implementing new but related work.

20. **Expertise**: I model respect of competency, honoring demonstrated skills, knowledge, work, and results.

21. **Fair-mindedness**: I believe in calmness and objectivity, using consistent standards so that my decisions and actions are fair, just, and effective.

22. **Fulfillment**: I want to concentrate my efforts on the dreams and endeavors that bring meaning and purpose to me and to those I lead.

23. **Harmony**: I work to keep conflict at bay so that people can concentrate on the tasks at hand.

24. **Individuality**: I value opportunities for solo efforts, making the most of each person's unique gifts, creativity, and inspirations.

25. **Influence**: I want to see my ideas, tools, or plans being used by others to create improvements, efficiencies, or significant change.

26. **Legacy**: I want to be involved in new ideas, paradigm shifts, or solutions to problems that others thought were difficult or even unsolvable.

27. **Loyalty**: I thrive when my skills, experience, and motivations are a long-term match to individuals, organizations, or causes.

28. **Mentoring**: One of my major responsibilities as a leader is guiding or supporting others in identifying their goals and developing their potential.

29. **Networking**: I am committed to making connections, sharing resources, and establishing relationships to enhance my team's effectiveness.

30. **Openness**: I seek and ponder contrary data, new perspectives, and other points of view before reaching conclusions.

31. **Optimism**: I want to inspire confidence in those I lead that our efforts will bring success.

32. **Organization**: I emphasize thinking through project or systems processes, needs, and expectations to create workable plans and practices.

33. **Originality**: I value tapping our imaginations, connecting ideas in unusual ways, and using artistic skills or other tools to find unique pathways.

34. **Personal development**: I am committed to continuous improvement of the skills and knowledge I and others need to reach our full potential.

35. **Perseverance**: I want to model and encourage others in sustaining momentum and having fortitude while making tangible progress.

36. **Promoting**: I work to advocate for needed resources and toot our horn externally.

37. **Relationships**: I invest time in building bonds with others for mutual support that can go beyond what might be required for the task at hand.

38. **Results**: Meeting or exceeding our stated goals is at the top of my priority list.

39. **Variety**: I thrive when my role involves a constant flow of new or novel activities, or many different kinds of activities.

40. **Visioning**: I believe in co-creating images of the future that motivate people and then leading them to work toward those common purposes.

Choosing ten priorities is a bit harder than it sounds, for as you read the priorities, you'll find that all have merit. Following are some of the questions people ask as they go about this task:

- **Why just ten?** Leadership is about focus. In most cases, being intentional about more than ten priorities would put an end to focus. In addition, priorities often act as criteria for decision making, so even ten can be difficult to manage when tackling a decision. If you are having trouble selecting your top ten, try ranking those you are considering from most to least important.

- **What if I would define the priority differently?** You'll see in a moment that these particular definitions tie tightly to the 12 Lenses for Leadership framework. For your top-ten list to be useful, use the definitions provided here. Feel free, however, to jot down your own definitions for later reference.

- **What if one of my core leadership priorities isn't listed?** Add your own priority to the list, but then set it aside and choose your top ten from the forty listed.

- **What if I have fewer than ten?** If you have fewer, then you're set! You'll be able to use the priorities you've chosen in the next step.

- **Wouldn't my priorities change depending on the situation?** Definitely. Leadership is situational. Your priorities depend on who you're leading, your tasks, the organization—in short, on just about everything. In fact, some of the reflection questions in this book will ask you to rethink your priorities with a different situation in mind.

Step 2: Align Your Priorities With Your Actions

Once you have determined your top ten leadership priorities, the next step is considering how they relate to the essential work of leadership. Intentional leaders go beyond identifying their values; they ponder how they will put them into action. We will be aligning your leadership actions with your priorities through what I call the *leadership lenses*. The twelve lenses each consist of two opposing tendencies that leaders need to balance—for example, the reality/vision lens and the planning/flexibility lens. Your core priorities define the lenses you tend to use most in your leadership actions. For example, leaders who choose *organization* as a priority usually devote time and resources to planning; however, without the opposing tendency of *adaptability,* a blind spot may be failing to adjust to changing circumstances.

Take a look at the 12 Lenses for Leadership on page 7. You'll see that each lens consists of two opposing tendencies that intentional leaders balance. Each lens is listed with its related leadership priorities (in italics). Find the priorities you chose as your top ten and highlight them on the chart. These priorities will help you evaluate which lenses you use—which components of effective leadership you tend to emphasize and which you might overlook. Use this table as your guide as you learn about the 12 Lenses for Leadership in chapters 3 through 14. Note which lenses are of most importance in your current role and which relevant priorities you might overlook. Then, as you read, you will be able to choose among the options contained in each chapter for how to develop each side of a lens to strengthen your approach to your current leadership role.

The Type and Emotional Quotient Connection

The 12 Lenses for Leadership come from an extensive review of research on the essential tasks and attitudes of successful leaders and how these tasks and attitudes relate to Jungian type preferences (Extraversion versus Introversion, Sensing versus Intuition, Thinking versus Feeling, and Judging versus Perceiving). Jungian type, or *personality type,* best known through the Myers-Briggs Type Indicator® (MBTI),[2] serves as a useful framework throughout this book for considering both what you do well and where you might naturally need more practice to use one of the twelve lenses effectively. The framework is explained thoroughly in chapter 2.

We'll also examine the impact of various aspects of emotional intelligence. We're all familiar with IQ—intelligence quotient. Back in 1980, Dr. Reuven Bar-On began work on an instrument to help people understand their *emotional quotient,* or EQ. Interest in the theory grew rapidly after Daniel Goleman published *Emotional Intelligence* in 1995, and the body of related research increased quickly as well. The second edition of Bar-On's instrument, EQ-i 2.0, came out in 2011.[3] Think of EQ as capabilities beyond cognitive abilities, specifically as "the ability to read the political and social environment, and landscape them; to intuitively grasp what others want and need, what their strengths and weaknesses are; to remain unruffled by stress; and to be engaging, the kind of person that others want to be around."[4]

Multiple models of EQ exist, but all of them discuss two broad components of EQ: (1) awareness of and ability to manage one's own emotions, and (2) awareness of and ability to manage the emotions of others. People who have an awareness of and the ability to manage their emotions:

> Can name whether they're angry, surprised, disappointed, frustrated or anxious, for example. Those who can't lump these emotions together as "angry." Being unable to identify all the nuances of emotions makes it harder to manage them; you end up with one-size-fits-all reactions to very different stimuli. Further, it's tougher to handle stress, to feel optimistic, or to purposely set and pursue a vision of success without feeling a connectedness that proper handling of emotions brings.[5]

The 12 Lenses for Leadership and Related Leadership Priorities

Lens 1	Outer Focus	Inner Focus
Priorities	Networking, Relationships	Individuality, Personal development
Lens 2	Breadth	Depth
Priorities	Variety, Influence	Depth, Legacy
Lens 3	Leadership	Listening
Priorities	Mentoring, Promoting	Empowering, Connecting
Lens 4	Reality	Vision
Priorities	Loyalty, Accountability	Visioning, Optimism
Lens 5	The Known	The New
Priorities	Experience, Creativity with the known	Challenge, Creativity with the new
Lens 6	Clarity	Ambiguity
Priorities	Efficiency, Dependability	Openness, Originality
Lens 7	Logic	Values
Priorities	Fair-mindedness	Empathy
Lens 8	Outcomes	People
Priorities	Results	Harmony
Lens 9	Individual Trust	Team Trust
Priorities	Expertise, Autonomy	Appreciation, Collaboration
Lens 10	Planning	Flexibility
Priorities	Organization	Adaptability
Lens 11	Goal Orientation	Engagement
Priorities	Achievement, Perseverance	Enjoyment, Fulfillment
Lens 12	Limits	Opportunities
Priorities	Balance	Discovery

Those who have an awareness of the ability to manage others' emotions:

> Can empathize so that others feel understood, are able to build trusting and satisfying relationships, and filter actions, plans and decisions through the concept of "the greater good."[6]

If there's a leadership position that doesn't require both of these components of EQ, chances are that it's within a workplace that requires you to lead without thinking for yourself, or without seeing another soul.

EQ isn't "soft stuff" or "fluff skills." Evidence is mounting that EQ counts more than IQ or talent for high-level executives since those with inadequate mental intelligence never even get to the top. EQ explains as much as 30 percent of the variance between successful and unsuccessful leaders when scores are compared on the EQ-i 2.0 and the Center for Creative Leadership's Benchmarks® multi-rater assessment tool, which looks at significant criteria for leadership success.[7]

EQ and personality type, along with the leadership priorities and the 12 Lenses for Leadership, will help you *intentionally*:

- Compare your own strengths and values to what is known about good leadership practices
- Pinpoint potential blind spots that might quickly become fatal flaws in your particular situation; every strength has a corresponding blind spot—a shadow side—and overuse has consequences
- Strategize to make the most of who you are

Why Bring Up Weaknesses?

Chances are, you've run across Gallup's research on strengths and the *StrengthsFinder 2.0* assessment.[8] This research concludes that we need to spend the majority of each day using our strengths and that trying to turn weaknesses into strengths takes more time and energy than it's worth. I agree.

However, all too often, this research is translated as, "We can *ignore* our weaknesses completely." That's a dangerous philosophy, especially for those in leadership positions. Why? Because strengths-based leadership is only half the story.

Recently, I was in a client meeting with several executive coaches. The client asked us, "You'll only be coaching our leaders on strengths, right?" One of the coaches, Doug Menikheim of Leadership Fingerprint, shook his head and said, "At their level, that would probably be a waste of time. Almost all top leaders have figured out their strengths—that's what took them to the top. In leadership coaching, it's not the strengths that need attention but weaknesses—shadow sides, zones of discomfort, areas of challenge."

Yes, we want to follow leaders who believe in their own abilities, but not leaders who are unaware of how they're likely to stumble. Further, for several reasons leaders often have a harder time being honest about their weaknesses than the people they lead. The Center for Creative Leadership notes four factors for this. First, people in power need to work hard to receive honest feedback. While anonymous 360-degree feedback processes often help, employees and even peers hesitate to point out a leader's flaws. Second, if the critique is delivered in a way that threatens the leader's feelings of competency, he or she may ignore it altogether—leaders want to believe in their own effectiveness. Third, because limiting the impact of a weakness often requires us to adjust how we use our strengths (think about pulling back from visioning to catch up on details), leaders fear they may lose the very edge that got them where they are. They worry, "I'm successful as I am; what if I change?" And finally, there's the nature of the job. Many leaders struggle to find time to reflect on what they are and aren't doing well.[9]

I find it helpful to use the term *blind spots* rather than *weaknesses*, for as you'll see in chapter 2, we're predisposed to view the world in certain ways, and those predispositions make it easy to ignore contrary viewpoints. Intentional leaders keep an eye on those blind spots and plan ahead. What does this look like? Here's a simple example.

When I took on the presidency of my international professional association, I consciously considered my priorities. One was to maintain the strong network of relationships I had with key members, sponsoring organizations, leaders in other countries, publishers, and other professional organizations as a way to keep our association strong. However, this priority goes hand-in-hand with one of my blind spots: I tend to assume that everyone is working for the greater good, sometimes forgetting that they also have their own interests to attend to. To manage my weakness, I asked two board members who were part of my network to please tell me if I failed to pick up on conflicts of interest or other key political concerns. Each of them found cause to do so at least once.

In his research on the characteristics of the companies that sustain superlative performance over many years, Jim Collins found that the eleven companies on which he focused all had similar leaders, whom he termed *level 5 leaders*: "an executive in whom genuine personal humility blends with intense professional will."[10] These leaders are motivated by ensuring the success of their organizations as well as their own personal success.

Humility allows us to not just acknowledge weaknesses but to *manage* them, which is key to developing leadership expertise. Sometimes you can leverage a strength, such as the network of colleagues on my association board who I counted on to bolster my political astuteness. But if you want to be an expert at key priorities for a given role, consider this conclusion from a compilation of over one hundred studies on how expertise is developed:

> When most people practice, they focus on the things they already know how to do. Deliberate practice is different. It entails considerable, specific, and sustained efforts to do something you can't do well—or even at all. Research across domains shows that it is only by working at what you can't do that you turn into the expert you want to become.[11]

The studies included those related to leadership; the researchers found that many of the key elements of leadership, such as charisma, can be learned through skilled coaching and deliberate practice.

Yes, you lead with your strengths. However, blind spots bring leaders down. Yes, building on strengths lets you become the best leader you can be, but intentional leaders also know that intentionally identifying and managing blind spots prevents them from becoming fatal flaws. Doing so means finding the right coach, the right strategies, or the right methods for practicing skills. Usually, it takes considerable effort to get to this point, because the term *blind spot* is very accurate—human beings are far better at spotting flaws in other people than they are in spotting their own.

The Hidden World of Weaknesses

For as long as philosophers have been philosophizing, they have agreed that we excel at ignoring our own weaknesses. You've probably heard at least one of these sayings before:

- "Knowing others is wisdom, knowing yourself is Enlightenment." —Lao Tzu

- "Men soon the faults of others learn. A few their virtues, too, find out; But is there one—I have a doubt—Who can his own defects discern?" —Sanskrit proverb

- "How can you think of saying, 'Friend, let me help you get rid of that speck in your eye,' when you can't see past the log in your own eye? Hypocrite! First get rid of the log in your own eye; then you will see well enough to deal with the speck in your friend's eye." —Luke 6:42, New Living Translation

- "Why do we judge others by their behavior and judge ourselves by our good intentions?" —Anonymous

Modern research shows that the ancients had it right—we *are* blind to our own flaws! In *The Happiness Hypothesis*, Jonathan Haidt summarizes, "The consistent finding of psychological research is that we are fairly accurate in our perceptions of others. It's our self-perceptions that are distorted because we look at ourselves in a rose-colored mirror."[12]

For those who think their capacity for self-assessment is above average, the results of current neuroscience are quite humbling. We don't even know what we know! Our brains are actually wired to jump to conclusions based on probabilities of being right rather than on certainties. As Kathryn Schulz points out in *Being Wrong*, life would be almost impossible if we didn't, for example, assume that the correct way to fill in the blank in "The giraffe had a long _____" is with "neck." (She suggests that other possibly right answers are "flight" or "history of drug abuse.") We can't take the time to thoroughly vet every piece of information we're given. But we don't consciously notice when we turn probabilities into facts.[13]

Further, once we've reached a conclusion, we tend to only look for evidence that supports it. We even fail to notice contrary evidence when it's right in front of us! In no area of knowledge are we so likely to be blind as in self-knowledge.

Jonathan Haidt relates the results of a Carnegie Mellon study on fairness during legal negotiations. If the participants knew before reading the case whether they'd be arguing for the defendant or plaintiff, they read the information in a biased way. Fully 25 percent failed to reach agreements, compared with 6 percent if they didn't know which role they would play. The researchers then tried several things to "de-bias" the participants. Reading an essay on self-serving biases helped participants better anticipate the actions of their opponents, but they did not adjust their own behavior or self-assessment of their fairness. If they wrote an essay about their opponent's point of view, it seemed to reinforce their own position. Only having to write an essay about the weaknesses in their own case seemed to lessen their biases. Indeed, the ancients had it right: we judge others and excuse ourselves.

When leaders do this, they're blind to the problems their blind spots are causing—and that's when events force those unintentional leaders to give me a call.

One unintentional leader told me, "My staff are just plain lazy. We have free rein to design our services any way we want, and they complain that it's too much work." She was shocked to hear that her staff complained to me. They asked, "Why hasn't she bothered to hunt down some examples that true experts created instead of making us reinvent the wheel?"

Another leader called, sure that her staff were resistant to change. It didn't take me long to discover that her strengths for finding new opportunities and novel ways of getting things done frustrated her staff because she didn't stick with initiatives long enough for them to bear fruit.

Then there was the unintentional leader whose excitement over future possibilities blinded him to the fact that his staff were overworked—and consequently facing health issues—in the here and now.

In nearly every case, the leader's blind spot provoked a crisis, triggering the call to me. My role is to listen to each member of the team, hear his or her side of the story, synthesize all the views, and then help the leader see how his or her overuse of particular strengths is fast becoming a fatal flaw.

Intentional Self-Knowledge

It's possible, though, to come to an honest understanding of what you do well as a leader and where your natural tendencies might produce difficulties as you work with and lead others. Let's look at what you need to be a good leader:

- **A willingness to be honest about your strengths and developmental needs**— What have you learned from past experiences? What sources provide you with honest feedback? Can you listen, reflect, and sometimes even laugh at who you once were and, even more important, who you are now? For example, because people today see me as a people-oriented, big-picture person, they often raise their eyebrows in disbelief when I mention that I started my career as a financial analyst. I thrived on the visionary projects we tackled, such as developing the first computerized systems for detecting deterioration in the condition of banking institutions. However, for my first six years in the industry, none of the analysts had personal computers, and for the first two years, spreadsheet software didn't exist. The detailed work of spreadsheets and batch entries definitely did not excite me. In fact, in putting through adjustment entries one Friday, I misplaced twenty-seven million dollars. The bank kinda wanted to know where it went. This experience and other similar ones made me keenly aware of my blind spot for details which now motivates me to partner with people who see what I miss.

- **A readiness to take responsibility for your actions and the results**—Especially in times of uncertainty, it's easy to blame circumstances or overall bad luck rather than figure out the role our own actions play in our circumstances. Intentional leaders look ahead, preparing to make the most of circumstances, good or bad.[14]

- **A commitment of time to the process**—Intentional leadership requires carving out time for reflection, comparing where you are to where you want to be and what might get in the way. Throughout these pages, you'll have opportunities to reflect deeply on the areas of leadership that will benefit most from your attention.

- **A method or a guide for being brutally self-honest**—Again, every "unintentional" call I've received is from a leader who has somehow gotten out of balance on one of the 12 Lenses for Leadership. These lenses, along with personality type and EQ, serve as your guide for self-evaluation and improvement.

The Plan

In this chapter, you identified your top ten leadership priorities. You used the chart on page 7 to identify the corresponding leadership lenses and discover your tendencies. Here's where you'll go from here:

- Chapter 2 explains personality type—your natural preferences for staying energized as a leader, gathering information, making decisions, and approaching your work. Identifying these natural preferences provides a neutral framework for thinking through being more intentional as a leader.

- Chapters 3 through 14 introduce the 12 Lenses for Leadership. Immerse yourself in these chapters. You can read them in order or start with a specific one. For example, begin with the one for which you highlighted the most corresponding leadership priorities, or start with one you hadn't thought about before, or choose the lens that seems most intriguing. Eventually, you'll want to read them all.

- Make a plan. Each chapter contains suggestions for improving your ability to use the lens. Choose and use the options you need to be more intentional in your current position.

Being intentional takes time, but that time is a worthwhile investment toward avoiding future problems that flow from being unintentional.

CHAPTER 2

A Framework for Strengths, Growth, and Those Pesky Pitfalls

Janson knew what an expert in psychological profiling would make of his dossier: the early history of betrayal and brutality that he had suffered. How deep did the trauma go, and could it be rekindled? His employers never referred to the possibility, but he could see it in their eyes; the personality inventory tests that he regularly underwent—the Myers-Briggs, the Thematic Apperception Test, the Aristos Personality Profile—were designed to ferret out any hairline fissures his psyche might have developed.[1]

This quote, from Robert Ludlum's *The Janson Directive*, describes what my most useful framework for leadership development—personality type—*isn't*! Yes, I'm a bit defensive. Wouldn't you be if you used a robust, well-researched framework that emphasizes the strengths inherent in all of us and promotes constructive use of the normal differences among people, yet you constantly saw it misused, abused, or misunderstood?

Truly, personality type says *nothing* about deviant behavior; I think Ludlum meant to refer to the Minnesota Multiphasic Personality Inventory (MMPI), which was designed to measure psychopathies. Other misunderstandings are also rampant: "It labels people," "It says you can only be one way or another," "It's a horoscope," and so on. While shallow or unethical use of type can lead to problems, my reason for centering my work on personality type is straightforward: I've never worked with a dysfunctional team where the core of the issues couldn't be approached via type; always, the framework played an essential role in helping the leader develop a successful course of action. Sometimes leaders overlooked an essential element of leadership that was opposite a key strength of people of their type. Other leaders misinterpreted the normal differences explained by type as deficits in their employees.

Type theory is backed up by decades of research and successful application. Further, Jung's model of eight mental functions, which are the basis for the sixteen personality types identified through the MBTI, is now validated by neuroscience.

Instruments such as the MBTI, Majors PTI, JTI, Insights, Golden Personality Type Profiler, and others, to say nothing of countless nonvalidated quizzes on the Internet, are useful in helping you self-select the type preferences that describe you best, but the real power comes through experiences that help you note patterns in normal, recognizable differences in people—differences that can keep leaders and team members from understanding and benefiting from each other's strengths. Type instruments are doorways, not answers. The benefits of using the concepts of type come from deep application.

Organizations that embed the framework of type in their culture have a robust schema for:

- Working through conflict
- Untangling problems and finding solutions
- Coaching and mentoring
- Supporting employee needs during change
- Sifting through what to keep, how to innovate, when to search more deeply, and when to simply take action

Type Defined

So what exactly is personality type? It is a framework for understanding differences in how people take in information (how we perceive) and make decisions (how we come to judgments). It isn't a labeling system but rather a dynamic system of psychological energy and processes.

Type theory doesn't predict what people will do. Instead, it describes what they *prefer* to do. Consider for a moment all the physical preferences we have. For example, sign your name on the line below.

_____

Most people say that doing so is easy, quick, and natural. They don't have to think about it. Now sign below with your other hand.

———————————

Most people find that using their nonpreferred hand is slow and awkward and requires a bit of thought. We *prefer* to use the other hand; it is one of our physical preferences.

Just about a hundred years ago, Swiss psychiatrist Carl Jung articulated his theory of psychological types, or personality preferences. Just like most people can sign their names with either hand, most people can use all of the mental preferences that Jung described—with practice. Just as we can practice writing, or dribbling a basketball, or playing the piano with either hand, we can practice improving our skills with all of the mental preferences. Maturity requires it of us, as you'll see.

The eight personality preferences are:
- Extraversion (E) and Introversion (I)
- Sensing (S) and Intuition (N)
- Thinking (T) and Feeling (F)
- Judging (J) and Perceiving (P)

Four of the eight preferences, one from each of the opposing pairs, come more easily for each of us, taking less effort and energy. Given all the energy that leadership requires, intentional leadership uses a framework to help you make the most of what you do well while heightening your awareness of where you can develop your skills. Let's explore the preferences in more detail.

How We Gain Energy for Leadership: Extraversion Versus Introversion

Jung began by pointing out that perhaps the most notable difference in personalities is whether we prefer to attend to the external or internal world.

- People who prefer Extraversion gain energy from action and interaction. They need activity or other people to do their best work and to find satisfaction in the day.
- People who prefer Introversion gain energy from solitude and reflection. They need time to reflect and process their thoughts to find satisfaction in the day.

In the past, the myth that the best leaders preferred Extraversion, exhibiting charisma and the ability to express ideas on the spot, permeated American business. However, the reality that people who prefer Introversion also excel at leadership is slowly being acknowledged. While this book was being written, *TIME, FORTUNE,*

Psychology Today, and *Scientific American,* among others, all published articles noting "groundbreaking" research demonstrating the positive results from Introverted leaders who seek contributions from everyone and take time to reflect before acting.

Use the chart that follows to identify your natural style. Remember that we develop skills that allow us to access either side, but one preference is more energizing and one is more draining. Also, since we develop skill with each of the preferences throughout life, think back to your late teen years to get clues about which is more natural to you. A preference for Extraversion or Introversion isn't about shyness or loving parties, but rather whether you need action and interaction to enjoy life or more time for solitude and reflection to stay energized. Which column best describes you?

Extraversion (E) When I prefer Extraversion, I am . . .	Introversion (I) When I prefer Introversion, I am . . .
Oriented to the outer world	Oriented to the inner world
Focusing on people and things	Focusing on ideas, inner impressions
Active	Reflective
Using trial and error with confidence	Considering deeply before acting
Scanning the environment for stimulation	Finding stimulation inwardly

From Gordon Lawrence © 1998. Descriptions of the 16 Types. *Gainesville, FL: Center for Applications of Psychological Type. Used with permission.*

Do you prefer Extraversion (E) or Introversion (I)? Note your preference on the line below.

———————

Once you step into a leadership role, keeping in mind your orientation toward Extraversion or Introversion is key to managing stress and optimizing decision making. Situations frequently force us to operate outside of our preferences—circumstances may require people who prefer Extraversion to work in isolation or take time to reflect, and people who prefer Introversion may have to interact with others or take less time for reflection than they would like. Leaders must be able to access both worlds.

Again, most people do both—in fact, to reach maturity, we need time in both our external and internal worlds. Otherwise we won't develop our preferred way of gathering information (referred to as our way of perceiving) or making decisions (referred to as our way of coming to judgments, or judging). This is the heart of the concept of balance within this framework. In chapters 3, 4, and 5, we'll examine leadership lenses that help you consider essential leadership tasks that involve both Extraversion and Introversion, and look at examples of executives who didn't realize that their environment called for them to access their nonpreferred sides. If you aren't sure which preference describes you best, the stories in those chapters may help you understand which is most natural for you.

How We View the World: Perceiving Through Sensing or Intuition

All of us perceive information day in and day out, but our preferred mental processes for perceiving information cause us to notice and trust different information. The two preferences are Sensing and Intuition.

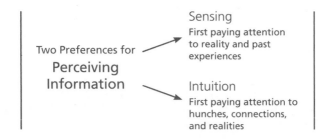

We "see" completely different information depending on whether we prefer Sensing or Intuition. Sensing types see the pieces, the facts, the aspects of reality conveyed through their five senses. Intuitive types see the whole, a synthesis of perceptions and conclusions. Again, as you look at the chart that follows, remember that mature people use both preferences, although not with equal ease and skill. To clarify your preferred way, think about what you notice *first* in new situations or with new information—the forest or the trees? Which column in the following chart best describes you?

Sensing (S) When using my Sensing, I am . . .	Intuition (N) When using my Intuition, I am . . .
Perceiving with the five senses	Perceiving with memory and associations
Attending to practical and factual details	Seeing patterns and meanings
In touch with the physical realities	Seeing possibilities
Attending to the present moment	Projecting possibilities for the future
Confining attention to what is said and done	Imagining; "reading between the lines"
Seeing "little things" in everyday life	Looking for the big picture
Attending to step-by-step experience	Having hunches, "ideas out of nowhere"
Letting "the eyes tell the mind"	Letting "the mind tell the eyes"

From Gordon Lawrence © 1998. Descriptions of the 16 Types. Gainesville, FL: Center for Applications of Psychological Type. Used with permission.

Do you prefer Sensing (S) or Intuition (N)? Write your preference on the line below.

_____

None of us can see the forest and the trees at the exact same time; our natural preference urges us to spend more time on the details or the big picture. Teams I've worked with that overemphasize Intuition have often pursued too many changes or initiatives. Teams that overemphasize Sensing haven't changed enough. And what if the team is split evenly? It is in conflict over how much should be changing. Chapters 6, 7, and 8 introduce leadership lenses that will help you access the essential leadership tasks of both Sensing and Intuition.

A Note on *Great by Choice*

In *Great by Choice*,[2] Jim Collins and Morten T. Hansen describe several strategies that are used by corporations that sustain continuous high performance through all circumstances. Note that several of the strategies are in essence methods for using both Sensing and Intuition wisely.

- **Zoom Out/Zoom In:** People use Intuition when they zoom out, taking in the big-picture view of the markets, economy, or competitors and grasping what is changing. People use Sensing to zoom in, taking a detailed look at how the organization might be affected. Companies that overemphasize Sensing, watching the realities of their own operations, can get caught flat-footed. Companies that overemphasize Intuition often bounce from one change effort to the next, with too little effort on a core business plan.

- **SMaC:** Collins and Hansen found that the great companies had specific, measurable, and consistent (SMaC) practices that worked in a wide range of circumstances. Identifying and preserving what works well is a general strength of those who utilize both Introversion and Sensing. Further, their tendency to insist on retaining "what works" is often viewed as resistance, and their advice is ignored by people with other preferences.

- **Bullets, then cannonballs:** Collins and Hansen describe how successful companies invest in research, looking for potential opportunities. However, when they find promising products, markets, or services, they test with small pilot efforts, or "bullets"; look for empirical evidence that they will be successful; and then determine whether the evidence supports firing "cannonballs," pursuing the opportunity on a large scale. Here, the search for new ideas involves Intuition, while the Sensing strengths base how to proceed on trials and evidence, not on hunches that a new idea will work. The comparison companies leaped into new markets or products without testing them.

How We Make Up Our Minds: Thinking or Feeling

We each have a preferred way of coming to judgments, or decisions, through the mental processes of Thinking or Feeling, as shown in the following diagram.

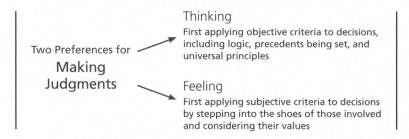

Two Preferences for
Making Judgments

Thinking
First applying objective criteria to decisions, including logic, precedents being set, and universal principles

Feeling
First applying subjective criteria to decisions by stepping into the shoes of those involved and considering their values

While most people use both kinds of criteria, they favor either the more objective or the more subjective style. People who prefer Thinking also have feelings and express emotions, and people who prefer Feeling can think—they are just as likely as Thinking types to be academically successful. However, we *prefer* one style over the other, especially when it comes to making decisions. Do you prefer Thinking or Feeling, based on the chart that follows?

Thinking (T) When reasoning with Thinking, I am . . .	Feeling (F) When reasoning with Feeling, I am . . .
Using logical analysis	Applying person-centered priorities
Using objective and impersonal criteria	Weighing human values and motives, my own and others'
Drawing cause-and-effect relationships	Appreciating
Being firm-minded	Valuing warmth in relationships
Prizing logical order	Prizing harmony
Being skeptical	Trusting

From Gordon Lawrence © 1998. Descriptions of the 16 Types. *Gainesville, FL: Center for Applications of Psychological Type. Used with permission.*

Do you prefer Thinking (T) or Feeling (F)? Write which you prefer in the blank below.

———————

If you aren't sure, consider how you handle making exceptions. Let's say an employee comes to you with a request to miss a mandatory meeting or to be exempt from a holiday shift requirement. Is your first thought to stick to the rules (Thinking), or are you more inclined to consider exceptions based on individual circumstances

(Feeling)? Great decisions use criteria from both Thinking and Feeling. Chapters 7, 8, and 9 provide leadership lenses for helping balance the essential strengths of these two mental processes.

How We Approach the External World: Judging or Perceiving

Isabel Briggs Myers, one of the creators of the MBTI, came up with the abbreviations for the type preferences (E, I, S, N, and so on). She added the Judging and Perceiving preferences to indicate how people function in the external world.

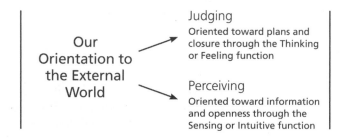

The concept of how this provides balance to our personality is described in the next section, but for now, consider which column in the chart best describes you.

Judging (J) When I take a Judging attitude, I am . . .	Perceiving (P) When I take a Perceiving attitude, I am . . .
Using Thinking or Feeling judgment outwardly	Using Sensing or Intuitive perception outwardly
Deciding and planning	Taking in information
Organizing and scheduling	Adapting and changing
Controlling and regulating	Curious and interested
Goal oriented	Open-minded
Wanting closure, even when data are incomplete	Resisting closure to obtain more data

From Gordon Lawrence © 1998. Descriptions of the 16 Types. *Gainesville, FL: Center for Applications of Psychological Type. Used with permission.*

Do you prefer Judging (J) or Perceiving (P)? Write which you prefer in the blank.

_____

Take a good look at the list for the Judging preference in the chart; in business culture in the United States, Judging is often considered *the* way to be—our workplaces and reward systems show that planning, organization, and timeliness are more accepted than a more flexible approach to work. Chapters 12, 13, and 14 examine the power of employing both preferences.

Your Four-Letter Type

Hopefully, you've now identified your four-letter type code, which you can record below.

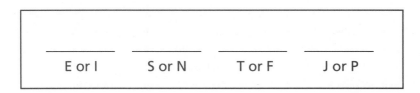

Once you've identified your four-letter type code, take a moment and read your type descriptions in the appendix (pages 151–167). Read the description for the type least like yours as well; you'll find it on the page facing your own type's description. The two descriptions describe very different leadership philosophies. Neither is better than the other, but rather each presents a unique approach with corresponding difficulties.

If you aren't yet sure of your four-letter code, know that reading through the stories in chapters 3–14 may help you decide on your style. Because intentional leadership is about using each of the type preferences as called for in given circumstances, you can use the 12 Lenses for Leadership without being sure of your own type preferences. However, the clearer you are, the easier it is to build a toolkit that can aid you in avoiding the common difficulties others of your type have experienced during leadership.

Balance in the World of Type

A better understanding of a balanced use of type often helps people affirm the type that fits them best. In Jungian type terms, balance has nothing to do with your score on an instrument such as the MBTI, or whether you spend equal amounts of time acting and reflecting. Instead, it's about:

- Spending adequate (not equal) time in the external and internal worlds
- Spending adequate (not equal) time gathering information (perceiving) and making decisions or coming to closure (judging)[3]

Have you ever worked with people who used a *perceiving* preference too much? Perhaps they seldom narrowed down priorities and spread themselves so thin that they struggled to fulfill commitments? They simply never came to judgments about which efforts are most key to success.

How about people who use a *judging* preference too much? They go with their first idea on almost every decision, refusing to consider new information once they make up their minds. Or, they decide based on first impressions of people, plans, and ideas. These people bypass perceiving other points of view or seeking new sources of information.

Of course, balance and imbalance are often misunderstood. As my colleague Hile Rutledge, head of OKA Inc., points out:

> Balance—and imbalance—are not static designations. They are flowing and ever-changing states. It is not realistic to proclaim someone a balanced individual, for the ebb and flow between perception and judgment [requiring both the inner and outer world] are ongoing. You can have a balanced morning but an overly judging (rigid and closed) afternoon. An overly perceiving discussion (meandering and procrastinating) can be followed by a balanced meeting. The effective flow between data gathering and decision-making is a constant goal—ever attainable yet always on the brink of slipping away.[4]

Jung observed that people perceive, through Sensing or Intuition, in the inner or outer world and judge, through Thinking or Feeling, in the other (and again, Myers added the last letters to the type code so that we could see this dynamic for each type). How does this work? Let's say that you perceive (taking in information through your preferred preference, Sensing or Intuition) when you're with others. In conversation, all kinds of ideas sound exciting or reasonable. Perhaps you even say, "Yes, I'll help with that." Then you get by yourself and realize you don't have time, or that you like a different idea more, or you otherwise regret speaking up. Your true position snaps into focus (coming to judgment through Thinking or Feeling) when you have time to yourself.

If you come to judgments with others, it's just the opposite. When you're alone, your mind processes all kinds of information and possibilities. Often, it's in talking with others that you suddenly decide which is best. The appendix (page 151) notes the perceiving and judging pattern for each preference.

What does type balance have to do with leadership? While effectiveness encompasses many more elements, most people agree that effective leaders are able to:

- Gather enough information before making a decision to ensure that they haven't overlooked important factors. In other words, they look for new resources or points of view.
- Come to a conclusion after they have gathered enough information. In other words, they make timely, but not rushed, decisions.

Thus, they can *perceive* the world and come to *judgments*. Those two processes are the essence of personality type. Isabel Briggs Myers et al. provide the following summary:

> Perception involves all the ways of becoming aware of things, people, happenings, or ideas. Judgment involves all the ways of coming to conclusions about what has been perceived. If people differ systematically in what they perceive and in how they reach conclusions, then it is only reasonable for them to differ correspondingly in their interests, reactions, values, motivations and skills.[5]

What You Can Do With Type

Understanding the types and your four-letter type code is just the beginning. Type lends patterns to human differences that let us:

- Use neutral language to discuss strengths and developmental needs
- Better interpret and utilize feedback from Executive Development 360 tools and other instruments
- Find tools and strategies that best fit each person's way of operating
- Predict, based on research, the needs of different team members and strategize to meet them

The type framework with its related tools and strategies developed over decades of application and research is simply too valuable not to use. Before delving into the 12 Lenses for Leadership, let's take a look at how type affects our needs during change.

Leaders, Change, and Type

"Help us get the resistors to change!" is a common request I receive, and type is a great tool for helping leaders see that changing the change process, not the resistors, is a better focus. Extensive research shows that there are clear differences in the information that people with different type preferences need during change, how they best process that information, the support they desire, and the factors that increase stress for them. When employees' needs aren't met, their resistance to change increases. Further, leaders in general fail to recognize and deal effectively with the needs of employees who don't share their type preferences.[6]

Take a look at the following chart and think through a recent change initiative in your organization that sparked resistance. Whose needs weren't met? Whose questions were never answered?

Questions for Considering the Needs of Each Preference During Change

Did people who prefer Extraversion have:	Did people who prefer Introversion have:
• Time for meaningful conversations regarding the changes? • Active roles in the process if desired? • Visible action steps and not just discussion about the changes?	• Information for reflection before being asked to respond or act? • One-to-one opportunities for both sharing thoughts and asking questions? • Time to internalize the meaning of changes before having to act?
Did people who prefer Sensing have:	**Did people who prefer Intuition have:**
• Real data that demonstrate why the change needs to be made and how it is better than the status quo? • Specific details regarding schedules, costs, and responsibilities? • Specific connections between the proposed changes, past practices, and other change efforts?	• The big picture—the underlying theories and long-term vision? • Options for implementation? • Opportunities to influence how the changes would be made?
Did people who prefer Thinking have:	**Did people who prefer Feeling have:**
• Logical explanations of how the new direction was chosen? • Evidence that leadership is competent in handling change? • Evidence of the fairness and equity of the proposed changes?	• Evidence that the changes were consistent with organizational values? • Plans that consider the values and needs of the people involved? • Processes that gave a voice to those most affected?
Did people who prefer Judging have:	**Did people who prefer Perceiving have:**
• Clear goals and time frames for the change process? • Clear priorities indicating what was and wasn't going to be done? • Assurance that surprises would be minimized?	• A plan that was open to changing goals and time frames as the process unfolded? • Processes for staying open to new information? • Flexibility for how each person would implement the changes?

Adapted from Differentiated School Leadership: Effective Collaboration, Communication, and Change Through Personality Type © *2008 by Jane A. G. Kise and Beth Russell. Thousand Oaks, CA: Corwin Press, p. 41.*

Further, as people plan for and initiate change, they have different priorities. In team workshops, I often conduct a simple exercise to demonstrate the differences in type. Participants form four groups based on their first two preferences: Introversion/ Sensing (I/S), Introversion/Intuition (I/N), Extraversion/Intuition (E/N), and Extraversion/Sensing (E/S). I ask them to write down on a flip chart how they would like to learn a new job. The flip chart papers have almost nothing in common! The I/S group wants clear instructions and opportunities for practice. The I/N group wants to explore policies and instruction manuals while working on a real task. The E/N group prefers to jump in and see what they need to know. The E/S group prefers shadowing someone in the job and asking questions.

Then, the team thinks through a change effort that didn't go well, using information similar to that found in the chart that follows, to experience how type can quickly provide key insights. In almost every case, the teams can see that they paid attention to some quadrants—the quadrants that the leader and a majority of the team prefer, for example—and ignored the others. We then work to intentionally put practices into place that incorporate the strengths and concerns of the neglected quadrants.

Change Concerns

Introversion and Sensing (I/S)	Introversion and Intuition (I/N)
If it's working, leave it alone!	*Let's think about change!*
• Value predictability, verifiable information, and sequential processes; the most thorough in change	• Value depth of understanding, creativity, and the chance to work on their ideas; the least practical in change
• Respect tradition	• Respect unique ideas for change
• Want to know why change is necessary	• Want to relate change to new concepts
• Need to relate change to what they know	• Need time to play with paradigm shifts
Stress is increased by change without careful planning or by endless conjectures about the future.	Stress is increased by change without opportunity for insights and creativity.
Extraversion and Sensing (E/S)	**Extraversion and Intuition (E/N)**
Let's just do it, not talk about it!	*Change? That'll make things better!*
• Value relevance, how change relates to the work they do; the most practical during change	• Value imaginative projects, minimal routine, and the big picture; the least thorough during change
• Respect tangible, useful results	• Respect creativity and innovations
• Want hands-on tasks, quick action	• Want leadership or planning roles
• Need to know how the changes will affect them tomorrow	• Need to relate change to the big picture
Stress is increased by change without tangible results or relevancy to their needs.	Stress is increased by demands that they do what they are told to do without question.

Type and Your Leadership Priorities

The following chart connects the type preferences to the 12 Lenses for Leadership. Again, highlight your top ten leadership priorities (in italics). Are there any preferences where you highlighted no priorities? If so, consider reading those chapters first; they may be worth more of your attention. Even if your current environment calls for a one-sided approach with some of the lenses (leaders in many manufacturing environments, for example, need to emphasize clarity over ambiguity), the lenses may alert you to unintended consequences or to more productive ways to move forward. The chapters are designed to help you consider the appropriate balance for each lens in a given environment and then intentionally plan for adjustments to your leadership style.

The 12 Lenses for Leadership aren't about using each side equally. Instead, they help leaders turn good intentions into great leadership by:

- Taking a big-picture view of essential aspects of leadership
- Focusing on what matters most where you are
- Pinpointing blind spots and development strategies to keep them from becoming fatal flaws in your role as a leader

Knowing that my own type preferences are INFJ, for example, validates my desire for more Inner Focus than Outer Focus. Yet the awareness of the opposite side of each of those lenses reminds me to set aside time for the networking essential to the groups and endeavors I lead. Type provides that essential link between who we are and the reality of the essentials of leadership so that we can be intentional about using our strengths to be the best leaders we can be.

The 12 Lenses for Leadership and Related Type
Preferences and Priorities

Type	Extraversion	Introversion
Lens 1	Outer Focus	Inner Focus
Priorities	Networking, Relationships	Individuality, Personal development
Lens 2	Breadth	Depth
Priorities	Variety, Influence	Depth, Legacy
Lens 3	Leadership	Listening
Priorities	Mentoring, Promoting	Empowering, Connecting

Type	Sensing	Intuition
Lens 4	Reality	Vision
Priorities	Loyalty, Accountability	Visioning, Optimism
Lens 5	The Known	The New
Priorities	Experience, Creativity with the known	Challenge, Creativity with the new
Lens 6	Clarity	Ambiguity
Priorities	Efficiency, Dependability	Openness, Originality

Type	Thinking	Feeling
Lens 7	Logic	Values
Priorities	Fair-mindedness	Empathy
Lens 8	Outcomes	People
Priorities	Results	Harmony
Lens 9	Individual Trust	Team Trust
Priorities	Expertise, Autonomy	Appreciation, Collaboration

Type	Judging	Perceiving
Lens 10	Planning	Flexibility
Priorities	Organization	Adaptability
Lens 11	Goal Orientation	Engagement
Priorities	Achievement, Perseverance	Enjoyment, Fulfillment
Lens 12	Limits	Opportunities
Priorities	Balance	Discovery

CHAPTER 3
Balancing Outer and Inner Focus

Lens 1

Extraversion	Introversion
Outer Focus	Inner Focus
Networking, Relationships	*Individuality, Personal development*

Traditionally, US businesses have rewarded the Extraverted, charismatic style of leadership. However, this is not the only effective style. Susan Cain, author of *Quiet: The Power of Introverts in a World That Can't Stop Talking*, traveled across the United States, looking for societal bias against Introversion. In an interview with *Scientific American* she said:

> One big [bias] is the notion that introverts can't be good leaders. According to groundbreaking new research by Adam Grant, a management professor at Wharton, introverted leaders sometimes deliver better outcomes than extroverts do. Introverts are more likely to let talented employees run with their ideas, rather than trying to put their own stamp on things. And they tend to be motivated not by ego or a desire for the spotlight, but by dedication to their larger goal. The ranks of transformative leaders in history illustrate this: Gandhi, Eleanor Roosevelt, and Rosa Parks were all introverts, and so are many of today's business leaders, from Douglas Conant of Campbell Soup to Larry Page at Google.[1]

Not only are the Introverted and Extraverted styles of leadership equally effective, but, as we learned in chapter 2, we all need to access both the inner and outer world to ensure we develop a mature way of taking in information (perceiving through Sensing or Intuition) and of making decisions (judging through Thinking or Feeling). We use our dominant function—whether Extraverted or Introverted—in our preferred world, and our auxiliary function in our nonpreferred world. Both worlds are vital to leadership.

- Leaders who underemphasize the tasks of Extraversion—too little outer focus—may fail to develop the networks and relationships vital to their group's work, may not convey their ideas, and may not be adequately aware of the needs of those they lead.

- Leaders who underemphasize the tasks of Introversion—too little inner focus—may not adequately reflect on information and experiences, may lack clear awareness of values and goals, and may not adequately use written forms of communication.

Let's look at Shane and Sara, two individuals who got out of balance.

Overly Outward Focus

For Shane, networking was at the top of his leadership priorities. A midlevel manager, he gave high priority to identifying and developing connections that might inform, support, or transform his team's efforts. Here's a sampling of his activities:

- A breakfast group he'd formed whose members were all his age and worked in a variety of industries

- A lunchtime book club that focused on reading business bestsellers

- Frequent "sharing" meetings with new contacts made through his network. After each person explained his or her expertise, they explored possible synergies

- High-profile lecture events sponsored by local universities and other organizations, to which Shane invited officers in his organization, vendors, and other contacts. They often said, "Without you, we would have missed this!"

- Cold calls to people in related industries that might in some way support his career or his team

- Regular meetings with his team, at which members were to report next steps with initiatives, as opposed to completed actions

There is no doubt that these efforts flowed from the strength Shane was most known for, keeping his team informed of cutting-edge information and a part of influential efforts.

Indeed, leadership requires looking outward. Consider who has the knowledge and resources your team might leverage. Which relationships will enhance your effectiveness? Think of all the avenues available for maintaining an outward focus: conferences, social media groups connected to your professional interests, alumni associations, service organizations, political groups, meetings with contacts in your industry, meetings with thought leaders in *any* industry—multiple opportunities any day of the week.

The authors of *The Innovator's DNA* expand the idea of networking to include the intentional actions of leaders who seek fresh ideas:

> Unlike typical delivery-driven executives who network to access resources, sell themselves or their companies, or boost their careers, innovators go out of their way to meet people with different backgrounds and perspectives to extend their own knowledge.[2]

In other words, excelling in your field requires focusing far beyond your field in a limitless quest to kindle excellence. Shane believed this, and his actions matched his beliefs.

Yet every moment spent looking outward steals from focusing inward to ensure that your actions and competencies are congruent with whom you intend to be as a leader. Shane, for example, wasn't digesting common threads of concern expressed by his team. The most significant one was, "Shane is constantly rushing us on to the next initiative before we've put one to rest. Last month, we were about 90 percent done with a great tool that other divisions in the company could have used to improve employee effectiveness, but before we could finalize the implementation process and how we would present it in management meetings, he moved us on. Yes, it *looked* done, but I bet we get 40 percent implementation, whereas if we'd polished it, 80 percent wasn't out of the question, it was so good. Even in our meetings, he only talks about what's next, not what's necessary."

The Type/Emotional Quotient Connection

Shane, whose networking activities reflected his Extraverted style, needed to spend time on the inward journey as well—to set priorities, objectively process feedback, and deliberately practice leading his team through implementation processes, not just innovation processes. Yet he *hated* sitting down to reflect.

Why? In part because the team's feedback concerning his lack of follow-through struck at the core of Shane's own self-doubts. Bouncing from one idea to another, Shane hadn't developed a clear picture of the expertise for which he wanted to be known. Without a target, his networking lacked focus; each new idea seemed more likely to help him strike gold. Once an effort had lost its novelty, he lost interest—especially with the unexciting tasks such as implementation.

The authors of *The EQ Edge* point out:

> Because individuals with healthy self-regard know their strengths and weaknesses and feel good about themselves, they have no trouble openly and appropriately

acknowledging when they have made mistakes, are wrong, or don't know all
the answers. Feeling sure of oneself is dependent on self-respect and self-esteem,
which are based on a fairly well-developed sense of identity.[3]

Shane didn't have a coherent picture of who he wanted to be, so any time he sat
still long enough to think about it, he felt he wasn't measuring up. So he didn't sit
still, didn't identify why his team's initiatives fell short of expectations, and didn't
engage in deliberate practice to better manage the great initiatives his strengths were
creating. The inward journey is integral to meaningful goals and deliberate pursuit
of the talents or skills essential to realizing them.

As a coach, my first move with clients like Shane is to assign reflection. I get them
to turn off phones and email alerts, close the door, and ponder some key questions.
Shane discovered patterns in how his efforts fell short of potential. This motivated
him to take a hard look at leading that last 10 percent of each project.

Overly Inward Focus

Let's meet someone with the opposite problem. Sara delighted in her role as division manager, having suffered through leaders who failed to follow through and
left her and others to make things happen. In fact, a replica of President Truman's
"The Buck Stops Here" sign sat right next to her phone and kept her focused on her
strategies for being intentional:

- To formulate plans and strategies to the best of her ability and then get input
  from her team to make them better
- To jump in when needed; for example, to understand each of her employee's
  roles so she could support them
- To practice the specific tools she and her coach had agreed upon for developing
  some key skills she needed for her position: receiving feedback constructively
  rather than personally, and meditating to keep stress under control

All of these are great strategies for leadership and development. The crucial inward
journey is as limitless as the outer journey: we can reflect on events and decisions,
take courses to improve skills or credentials, work with a coach, read the latest
research and theory, or identify and then dedicate time to overcoming a blind spot
or trouble area that could hold us back. Only through the insights that reflection
makes possible can we continue to lead from our strengths, yet spot our fatal flaws,
and then engage in deliberate practice of skills and strategies to keep them from
undermining our leadership intentions.

Sara, though, was so focused on her inward journey that she failed to gather outside input. She felt that networking took her away from the essence of her leadership
tasks. She had even internalized networking as selfish career-building that kept her

out of the office—an impression reinforced by a former manager who seemed to spend more time looking for the next step up in his career than on his current job.

She dismissed feedback from her team that she developed plans without them; the team's perception couldn't be accurate because she consistently asked for members' input once she drafted plans. She didn't realize (because she hadn't asked) that her plans had a polished look that discouraged the input she sought. When she participated hands on to ensure that the team met a deadline, she dismissed comments such as, "We can finish this—isn't it keeping you from coordinating resources for our next project?" She assumed her coworkers were either being polite or resented the implication that they couldn't handle the task; however, one of her managers pointed out clearly inappropriate help that Sara offered when she commented, "Sara actually made copies for the final meeting when she could have been getting her peers on board with the agenda. What a waste!"

The Type/Emotional Quotient Connection

Sara's natural inclination toward Introversion caused her to get too caught up on her inward developmental journey. Concentrating so intensely on becoming the leader she wanted to be, Sara forgot to pay attention to what others needed from her. Her failure to take others' perspectives into account showed a lapse in her use of the EQ competency of understanding the emotions of others.

With a client like Sara, my first move is getting him or her to act and interact with his or her employees. In Sara's case, we decided to hold a planning meeting on the next project where she shared ideas—not a full plan. She was amazed at how much more valuable input she received when employees believed she wanted their ideas!

Using the Outward/Inward Focus Leadership Lens

The essential nature of this lens, which examines whether you spend *enough* time on the outer and inner journeys, becomes apparent when you review some of the most important EQ competencies for leaders.[4] These include empathy and social responsibility, both of which require an outer focus, as well as emotional self-awareness and self-actualization, both of which require an inner focus. What these EQ competencies tell us is that leaders need to make space for action *and* reflection, and interaction *and* solitude.

While Shane's and Sara's imbalances on this lens might seem a bit extreme, their stories illustrate how views on the outward and inward journeys are crafted by values and past experiences that can blind leaders to the value of the other side of the lens.

Let's look again at the leadership priorities connected with the outer focus/inner focus leadership lens to grasp how to balance these needs in your current role. Begin by highlighting any in the following chart that are on your top-ten list.

Outer Focus	Inner Focus
Networking	*Individuality*
I am committed to making connections, sharing resources, and establishing relationships to enhance my team's effectiveness.	I value opportunities for solo efforts, making the most of each person's unique gifts, creativity, and inspirations.
Relationships	*Personal development*
I invest time in building bonds with others for mutual support that can go beyond what might be required for the task at hand.	I am committed to continuous improvement of the skills and knowledge I and others need to reach our full potential.

Are you more like Shane, or are you more like Sara? Which of the following opportunities excite you more? Do you prefer:

- Time to exchange ideas with a variety of people (like Shane), or time to ponder your own ideas, goals, and needs (like Sara)?
- Moving out and about through the office (like Shane), or working productively behind closed doors (like Sara)?
- Getting to know employees personally (like Shane), or spending time with a coach (like Sara)?

Remember, equal time isn't the goal, but rather spending enough time focusing both outwardly and inwardly to be effective as a leader. Considering these different options, where would you place yourself on the following scale—more like Shane or more like Sara?

The following questions are designed to help you think through your current activities. Are you spending enough (not necessarily equal) time in the outer and inner worlds? Once you have read through items one and two, you will be asked to go back and rate your time spent with each activity using the blank spaces provided.

1. Which of the following outward focus activities do you engage in regularly?

    a. Informal meetings with other leaders in my organization or industry
    _____

    b. Vehicles for networking that provide opportunities for new connections
    _____

    c. Regular professional organization or association meetings _____

   d. Leadership roles within professional associations _____

   e. Expanding my social media networking through Facebook, LinkedIn, Twitter, and so on _____

   f. Meeting with people from other cultures and industries _____

   g. Attending conferences _____

   h. Spending time with colleagues and coworkers *not* dedicated to the task at hand _____

   i. Nurturing key relationships _____

2. Which of the following inward focus activities do you engage in regularly?

   a. Purposely scheduling reflective time after important meetings or decisions _____

   b. Reflecting on your goals and personal development needs _____

   c. Meeting with a coach or mentor _____

   d. Learning opportunities to develop or enhance specific skills (formal courses, webinars, workshops, and so on) _____

   e. Journaling or reflecting before making a big decision _____

   f. Defining what is most important to you and reflecting on whether your current path will get you where you wish to go _____

3. Ponder your responses to questions one and two in light of your current situation or the leadership role you would next like to undertake. Are you properly balancing having an inward and outward focus? Why? What evidence supports your opinion? You might even check your response with someone you trust.

4. Look through the activities again in questions one and two. In the spaces provided after each item, make one of the following marks:

   ↑ (I could do more of this.)

   ↓ (I could do less of this.)

   ✓ (I'm doing the right amount.)

5. Of the items you think you could do more of, choose one or two. Set some goals for increasing the time you spend on each one.

Coaching Yourself as an Intentional Leader

Before considering the options for developing your ability to use the outer/inner focus leadership lens:

- Get specific about your goals so that you choose wisely. For example, are you—
  - Developing a specific EQ competency involving your own emotions or those of others?

- Increasing your awareness of one of the leadership priorities that wasn't in your top ten?
- Working on a specific skill such as networking?

- If it's been a long time since you've taken stock of who you are versus who you want to be, consider your goals for the inner journey. Are you clarifying your goals? Are you satisfied with life? Is your main interest reflecting on your effectiveness?

- Check your type page in the appendix (page 151) to make any adjustments for the way you learn best, but also consider embracing an opportunity to stretch.

Options for Developing an Outer Focus

Attend a workshop. Pick a workshop on a topic that truly interests you, related to your professional goals or your team's needs. Make sure, though, that it won't just be "sit 'n' git." Check whether seating will be at round tables or auditorium style with little chance for interaction. If lunch is included, try to sit with people who you thought made interesting contributions earlier in the day.

Often, local branches of national or international professional associations offer reasonably priced workshops. When I first set out to become a published writer, I checked listings with several groups and chose a two-day workshop. At that first event, I met people from several organizations, learned about their programming, and soon joined the one that seemed to best suit my needs. I made several key connections that I still maintain today.

Join a professional organization. As someone who prefers Introversion, this is one of my favorite ways to network when I need to expand connections into new areas of expertise. Right now, I belong to at least seven professional organizations, and in some cases, both the local and international groups. Within the local groups, consider taking a leadership role; few of these groups have enough volunteers, yet the leaders often have an extensive network of contacts and, in my experience, are willing to help other volunteers make connections. Ask around—which groups do your peers belong to? Check the Internet; often, groups that have savvy websites also have savvy members and worthwhile meetings.

Stretch your gregariousness. On the more detailed MBTI Step II™ report[5] there's a scale for *gregarious* (preferring to associate with a wide variety of people) and *intimate* (preferring fewer relationships and one-on-one conversations). If you'd say your preference is for intimate, consider these suggestions:

- Set a goal of knowing a few things about each person you work with that can supply nonwork topics for casual conversation. What sports do their children play? Are they interested in sharing book titles? Find a connection.

- Before a networking function, scan the newspaper for a few topics that might slip easily into conversation. "What did you think of . . ." or "I noticed this morning that . . ." are natural conversation starters.

- Volunteer for group efforts at work or outside of work. These events are a natural environment for asking questions, which is an easy way to build relationships. Some people even find it easier to practice conversation skills with strangers, so they initiate conversations on airplanes or in grocery checkout lines!

Focus on the collegial side of the workplace. While many of us like to keep our personal lives to ourselves, having fun together often enhances teamwork as coworkers see each other's skills in a new light. Although happy hours are often the default choice, other very successful options I've seen include the following:

- Meeting for a series of potluck lunches. At one office, people signed up for bringing a salad, main course, or dessert, and the group gathered to watch a classic or comedy movie over the course of a week's worth of lunches.

- In another office, each department made a minigolf hole in their area. The office closed early one evening and everyone played the course together.

- Consider organizing lunchtime power walks (see chapter 12, page 117, for insights into how this boosts overall productivity).

- Arrange fun contests such as best chocolate dessert or healthy appetizer—judging is fun!

- One office had a Thursday morning "sacred donut hour." If you were meeting with clients, they needed to attend, too. Supplemented with apples for those who wanted to avoid temptation, it was an opportunity to take a once-a-week pause to catch up with everyone.

Options for Developing an Inner Focus

Reflect on your leadership priorities. When you chose your top ten priorities in the previous chapter, you did so with a specific leadership position in mind. Are these priorities congruent with your goals for:

- Your personal life?
- Your professional development goals?
- Your image of an ideal leader?

Are there any incongruencies? Do you need to make any adjustments to stay on track with who you want to be in all aspects of your life?

Take the long route home to reflect. Leadership and time for reflection sometimes seem to be mutually exclusive. Carve out some solitude by driving or walking alone to meetings. On the return trip, resist the temptation to make phone calls. Instead, reflect on your reactions to information you heard and decisions that were made. Or, take a few minutes to reflect while still in the parking lot after a meeting. Use a dictation app on your smartphone or tablet to record thoughts and questions while the conversations are still fresh in your mind.

Name or reframe the problem. Make a practice of revisiting your first impressions to ensure a presenting problem is the real issue. For example, after a key teambuilding session, one of my clients said that she was satisfied with the respect her employees were developing for each other. The next day, though, she called me to say that while looking back through her notes, she realized that one of her direct reports offered several compliments that discounted his own value to the team. He seemed to think that three other team members with similar personalities were somehow superior to him. She noted that this simply was not true. These insights inspired specific conversations with the team about being able to articulate their own unique value as well as that of their coworkers.

Choose a reflection activity. Choose an activity for reflection and add it to your schedule. You might, for example, set aside time each Friday afternoon to write out two actions you will take to meet a goal or reflect on your actions in light of your ten leadership priorities. Some of my clients have breakfast monthly with an accountability partner to reflect on goals they shared at the last meeting.

> Remember, the outward/inward leadership lens helps you evaluate how you are managing the work of action and interaction with the work of solitude and reflection in your current environment. Have you found the right balance?

CHAPTER 4

Balancing Breadth and Depth

Lens 2

Extraversion	Introversion
Breadth	Depth
Variety, Influence	*Depth, Legacy*

Would you rather know a lot about a few subjects or a little about a lot of subjects? An individual's preference for breadth or depth and how he or she gets ideas is tied to preference for Extraversion or Introversion. My colleagues who prefer Extraversion tell me that when they're stuck coming up with ideas, they might broaden their perspective by:

- Heading to the Mall of America, Grand Central Station, or an employee cafeteria, where the variety of sights, sounds, and people spark their creative process

- Calling or having coffee with friends who enjoy tossing around ideas

- Scanning the magazine racks at a local bookstore or their Twitter feed to see what topics seem to be trending or what new publications are catching on

Variety helps Extroverts spot what's new, what's different, and thus where they might turn next.

My colleagues (and I!) who prefer Introversion proceed quite differently. We might deepen our understanding of a subject by:

- Closing the office door and staring at our books until an idea pops into our heads

- Surfing relevant research on the web or getting a new stack of relevant books from the library to read
- Sitting by ourselves while journaling about a core idea in a favorite neighborhood coffee shop, headphones piping some favorite music

Do you thrive on variety and interaction or on depth and concentration? In your current role, is pursuing a variety of projects or leads or sources valued—or is concentrating in depth more important? Which emphasis is consistent with your own motivations? This orientation spills over into how we approach all of our work.

Leaders who overemphasize breadth may assume that everyone thrives on ever-changing activities, signing their teams up for a smorgasbord of special projects or professional development initiatives. Leaders who overemphasize depth may assume that no one is eager to explore more initiatives.

Variety can definitely lead to cross-pollination, where ideas from one effort spark innovation in another. Minds stay fresh through information about late-breaking developments. Done well, variety allows leaders and teams to spot and incorporate brand-new tools and trends that can immediately influence how things are done.

However, leaders who like breadth and variety may move away from things too quickly. At its worst, this style can rob employees of motivation. As Daniel Pink points out in *Drive*,[1] the opportunity to master something, to develop expertise, is one of three key factors that truly motivate employees, along with autonomy and a sense of purpose. Mastery, though, takes intense practice over a long period of time. At the extreme, variety leaders change priorities so often that their teams assume they needn't bother mastering anything—their efforts will be wasted once the next new thing pops up.

The upside of depth is the chance to pursue mastery. However, imbalance caused by too much focus on depth can lead to just as many problems as too much variety, notably through a "purist paralysis" that stymies the whole team or even the leader's career. Perhaps a chosen expertise is so narrow that it becomes obsolete. Or, mastery is defined with an impossible level of foolproof perfection. Meanwhile, someone else corners the market or fills the niche.

Managing breadth and depth well often allows leaders to live up to their potential, the EQ skill of *self-actualization*, one of the seven EQ competencies cited as essential to leadership.[2] People who rate well on this quality have identified worthy, deep goals and are willing to work hard on the tasks or skills it takes to reach them. Using the breadth/depth leadership lens well also fuels optimism; breadth provides a multitude of options while depth builds confidence that you can accomplish what you set out to do.

Still, some of us are more wired for depth, focusing for mastery, and others for breadth, exploring multiple ideas, innovations, or responsibilities. In *Good to Great*, Collins reflects on a line by Greek poet Archilochus: "The fox knows many things, but the hedgehog knows one big thing." Hedgehogs use their single defense trick of rolling into a prickly ball no matter what wiles the fox tries. Collins notes that companies need to find their "hedgehog"—that intense focus on what they do well.[3]

History, though, tells us that individuals can thrive either way. Isaiah Berlin divided great writers and philosophers, for example, into foxes who explore a multitude of ideas and hedgehogs who understand, think, and feel through a single organizing principle. His foxes include Shakespeare, Aristotle, Goethe, and Joyce, and his hedgehogs Dante, Dostoevsky, Ibsen, and Proust.[4] It'd be great to be on either list, wouldn't it!

Of course, everyone in Berlin's hall of fame was in a sense a hedgehog as either a writer or philosopher. Intentional leaders also have their hedgehog of leadership, yet some seek a variety of positions and industries while others prefer to stay closer to a core expertise.

Which are you? And are you leading natural hedgehogs or natural foxes? Does your current environment require one, the other, or both? Let's consider Leah and Loren.

Too Much Variety

When Leah took over as vice president of manufacturing for a midsized firm, she knew that things needed shaking up a bit. Her predecessor had retired from the position after almost twenty years, and Leah's boss told her, "It's perhaps no surprise that things have stagnated. I want your team to start leading the way. Where can they be industry pioneers?"

One of Leah's first moves was to find out how long each of those who reported directly to her had been in his or her current position—an average of nine years, with some as long as fourteen. She couldn't imagine doing the same thing for so long. She located the organization chart file on her computer, opened it, and systematically moved each person to a new position. Surely after all these years of working together, they know enough about each other's responsibilities to change places, she decided.

Then she called them all together. "This is my gift to you," she began as she handed out copies of the updated organization chart. "As you explore your new responsibilities, with fresh eyes on each other's resources and fresh possibilities within your existing networks, you'll unearth different opportunities. Here are your three guiding questions for the shift:

1. **"Why are we doing things the way they're being done?** I'm not assuming the current ways are wrong, but rather asking you to examine any practices for which this question has no clear answer.

2. **"What has been out there during the last twelve months we might have missed?** Think about who might be doing it better than we are and what new customer needs exist that could be filled

3. **"What if this were different?** Maybe it's blasé to ask you to think outside the box, but that's what I have in mind. What if something were bigger? Smaller? Done by machine? Done by hand?"

Leah continued, "Don't worry—I'm not going to micromanage your transitions. Work together to figure out how and when you can transfer responsibilities and let me know your plans. I know these changes call for extra time for you to meet, so I'll fend off requests from other departments until you're set."

What happened next? A few managers were excited by their new responsibilities. A few were terror-stricken—how could they lead without the deep expertise they'd developed in their current areas? Their employees knew more than they did now! One or two headed straight to human resources to check on early retirement possibilities. Before a year had passed, Leah recognized that while a few areas had benefited, an equal number seemed more stagnant than before.

The Type/Emotional Quotient Connection

If Leah's story seems a little far-fetched, it's not. I've worked with three organizations where a leader made this move, changing managers around so that many no longer felt grounded as leaders in their own area of expertise. In each case, the leaders believed that people become stagnant if they stay in the same place for too long. Leah didn't take time to build trust or to get to know her managers. Her natural preference for Extraversion pushed her toward action without reflection on other options for re-energizing her new team.

The EQ skill of *empathy*, which involves not just understanding the emotions of others, but being able to articulate them in ways that demonstrate that understanding, might have helped Leah identify which of her employees were hedgehogs and which were foxes. Picture what might have happened if Leah had gotten to know her team first. Yes, her management had grown complacent, and reorganization was perhaps a good strategy, but spending time to build relationships allows for providing the very different kinds of support people need during change.

Now let's examine what happens when leaders seek too much depth.

Too Much Depth

Ask anyone in Loren's company, "Who knows the most about creating solid leadership development programs?" and they'd say, "Loren, of course." Besides implementing stellar initiatives, he spoke at conferences, wrote articles for his professional association, and mentored those around him in solid knowledge and techniques.

Loren's methods centered on a model he had developed through years of study and experimentation. Others urged him, "Get it into a book!" In fact, Loren's company felt that his ideas were so significant that it had assigned additional employees to his area to assist him in making the book a reality. Loren, though, felt that he and his team needed to complete a couple of significant research pieces before putting the model into a format that others could use. They were following up with several cohorts of leaders he'd trained to determine which aspects of his model still had an impact years later. This study also conveniently provided data on how fast these individuals were promoted, their responsibility level, and other key information.

Finally, someone in management asked Loren, "When will we see the final project?"

"Well, my vision has always included the twenty-year longitudinal study. And of course with what we've gleaned from it so far, I've been modifying the model and want to test . . . ."

"You're kidding, right?" his colleague interrupted. "You've got a proven program—proven through years of implementation—and you don't think it's good enough yet?"

The Type/Emotional Quotient Connection

Loren, with his natural preferences for Introversion and depth, was intrinsically fascinated by his model and could still see ways to improve it. However, he had lost perspective. While it could be improved, at what point was it truly good enough?—especially since, as even his employees were trying to tell him, it was truly a great working model!

Loren needed to develop a stronger appreciation of his strengths and expertise. His own lack of confidence kept him from believing that there was more than one way to validate the great work he and his colleagues had developed. While he was certainly right to continue his research, the empirical evidence of the program's success should have been sufficient to convince him it was ready for publication. After all, a second edition could always include the final research results. Further, perhaps reflecting on his preference for Introversion, he'd chosen to gather data through surveys, not through interaction; if he'd met face-to-face with his successful graduates, their enthusiasm might have increased his confidence in the value of his work.

Using the Breadth/Depth Leadership Lens

Because Extraversion and Introversion describe the activities that keep us energized, using the breadth/depth leadership lens well increases the chance that both you and your team can direct energy toward the tasks at hand rather than toward managing the environment.

The leadership priorities connected with this leadership lens appear in the following chart. Highlight any that are on your top-ten list.

Breadth	Depth
Variety	*Depth*
I thrive when my role involves a constant flow of new or novel activities, or many different kinds of activities.	I want to be in charge of long-term, significant projects where we pursue a major goal or develop important expertise.
Influence	*Legacy*
I need to know that my ideas, tools, or plans are valued or used by others to create improvements, efficiencies, or significant change.	I want to be involved in new ideas, paradigm shifts, or solutions to problems that others thought were difficult or even unsolvable.

Are you more like Leah, or are you more like Loren? Consider your actions and attitudes over the past five years:

- Are you known for a variety of general talents (like Leah) or a deep expertise (like Loren)?
- Do you get restless in the same position (like Leah), or do you consider a long-term position a gift for thorough exploration (like Loren)?
- Do you like to have a direct impact in the here and now (like Leah), or are you working on something that would have a lasting impact in your field (like Loren)?

What would your employees say about your breadth and depth and the effects it has on them? Do they have ample opportunity to develop deep expertise? Might they complain of stagnation? Considering these different options, where would you rate yourself on the following scale—more like Leah or more like Loren?

Coaching Yourself as an Intentional Leader

Before considering the options for improving your use of the breadth/depth leadership lens, do the following:

- Identify your goals. For breadth, are you working to avoid stagnation? To take advantage of new opportunities? To be on the cutting edge, a current influencer? To develop more general expertise in order to qualify for a wider variety of positions? For depth, are you searching for a goal or competency worthy of intensive effort over time? Are you seeking a level of expertise for which you might be recognized?

- Regarding EQ, note that too much self-confidence can keep us from listening to others since we can assume we know what they want or need. Empathy is not only a top EQ skill for leaders, but it is also key in balancing self-management and managing the emotions of others. How does empathy affect your use of the breadth/depth leadership lens?

Options for Increasing Breadth

Explore variety. Follow the lead of variety-seeking Extraverts through at least one of these activities:

- Scan magazine racks for trends. How do they relate to your business?

- When you're at the airport, observe what people are doing and consider how it relates to your responsibilities.

- Identify five experiences, trainings, or volunteer or task-force roles that are out of the ordinary for you yet related to your professional development goals. Choose one, and then consider what new connections, ideas, or insights you gained through doing something different.

Explore other contexts. Set aside the "cant's" and think through how your expertise might be useful in medicine, journalism, health care, with your favorite volunteer opportunity, and so on. Go online and look at conference presentations to research who is doing what with your knowledge. You may never use it in these fields, but you might discover new ways to use it where you are.

Pass on your expertise. What have you mastered that you could teach to others? What are you doing that no one else is? Could you team with a university on action research or to teach courses, become active in a professional association, write articles, or work with someone with different expertise to create something new? All of these could increase your circle of influence.

Ask employees where they might leverage what they know. Set a goal of each team member finding one area where better processes, products, or knowledge are needed. How might they learn more, experiment, innovate to improve their own results, and then influence their field?

Read, watch, and attend with variety. Avoid the rut of attending only one conference, reading only journals connected directly with your expertise, or sticking to the same nonfiction topics. Instead, read from other fields. What connections can you make? Go to www.ted.com and watch some of the less-than-twenty-minute talks from experts (in nearly every field). What might you learn from Jane Goodall, high school math teacher Dan Meyer, leading authors, biologists, entrepreneurs in technology companies, and more?

Options for Increasing Depth

Unite your favorite pursuits. Is there an area for growth that you've kept as a top priority for more than five years? It could be a particular topic where you keep up on the latest literature, your own research interest, or a theory, framework, or model connected to your profession. If you *don't* have one, how might this lack of a priority be hurting you? If you do have one, when did you last evaluate whether you are giving it more or less attention than it deserves?

Make a list of at least ten fulfilling tasks, projects, experiences, or responsibilities you've been part of over the past five years. Consider work, education-related projects such as research, and volunteer efforts. For each, write down the following:

- Why you got involved
- Why it was fulfilling
- The skills, tasks, or special knowledge you put to use

Then, look for patterns in your motivations, results, unexpected benefits, and so on. What fires you up? In what might you invest more time for development?

Consider how others view you. Ask people who know you well to name your strengths. One way to phrase it is, "If you are asked, 'Who do we know that can _____,' when does my name come to mind?" Consider using SurveyMonkey® (www.surveymonkey.com), an easy-to-use, confidential survey tool, if you are worried about not receiving honest answers.

Then evaluate the results. Have you mastered the skills, talent, or knowledge they mention? Where might you employ deliberate practice to develop more expertise? Are you interested in making that commitment? What might be the benefits? One goal here is developing self-confidence. How can you build confidence in your ability to have a lasting impact?

Evaluate team opinions. Sit down with your team to consider members' overall depth of expertise. Framing the exercise as a tool for investigating possible professional opportunities for everyone, ask team members in which circumstances they feel as though they operate in "flow"—that their knowledge and skills meet the challenge so they are fully engaged. Where do they sense that processes slow down and why? Where might expertise be added to the team? When, given more time, might they have made further innovations, contributions, efficiency improvements, or otherwise seen quality improvement via depth? What actions should the team take to acquire more depth?

Study depth. Find role models who are somehow related to your own work. Who are the experts? How did they develop that expertise? How do they keep their talents cutting-edge? For example, I recently gained new strategies and insights for my own writing by reading *MetaMaus*. The book details how Art Spiegelman created *Maus* and *Maus II,* his Pulitzer Prize–winning masterpiece in graphic nonfiction that retells his father's Holocaust experience. Even though my writing plans don't include graphic novels, I learned from Spiegelman's research strategies, illustration and layout choices, negotiation between historical facts and his father's memories, and his battles with others' misunderstandings of the work.

Read *Bonhoeffer* by Eric Metaxas to understand the depth of study, analysis, and commitment that Dietrich Bonhoeffer invested in influencing the Church in Germany to oppose Hitler and his eventual decision to join the plot to assassinate him. Study the expertise of the leaders identified in *Great by Choice* whose organizations far outperformed competitors through good times and bad.

All of these are humbling examples of depth that leaves a lasting legacy.

Consider the Google 20 percent practice. Google allows employees to spend up to 20 percent of their time on an initiative related to company business that forms out of their own interests and ideas. If your company adopted such a policy, on what effort might you spend 20 percent of your time? Consider how you might allocate at least some time to this idea. With enough foundational work, you might be able to pursue it at a deeper, satisfying level.

> Remember, the breadth/depth leadership lens helps you balance the excitement of variety and current opportunities with depth and having a lasting impact. Does your current environment respect both?

CHAPTER 5

Balancing Leadership
With Listening

Lens 3

Extraversion	Introversion
Leadership	Listening
Mentoring, Promoting	*Empowering, Connecting*

Almost every leader can name at least one mentor who enriched his or her career path. Who comes to mind for you? Intentional leaders understand that they serve in some capacity as coach to their employees, providing skill-development opportunities and support for current roles and natural career progression. But they also understand the importance of mentoring, which requires a different time commitment, a great match in interpersonal dynamics, and a common understanding of aspirations.

Mentoring is not a recent phenomenon. Over 3,000 years ago, the Greek Odysseus chose his wise colleague, Mentor, to watch over his household—and in particular, over his beloved son Telemachus. In *The Odyssey*, Mentor speaks up only after his charge asks the assembly of Ithaca for help in ridding his father's household of the suitors who hope to snag his mother and who are eating them out of house and home. At the end of the story, Mentor turns out to be Athena, the goddess of wisdom, in disguise.

Then, about 300 years ago, the French author Fénelon, tutor to an heir to the throne of France, made Mentor the hero of his book, *The Adventures of Telemachus*. In Fénelon's story, Mentor takes the young boy on a sea journey, using the days to impart his wisdom on being a king.

The difference in how these two stories portray Mentor's role—guiding as needed or working to shape the mentee's values and beliefs—is right at the heart of what it means to be a good mentor. The mentoring side of leading takes careful thought. Formal mentoring between a person with considerable experience in a field and a protégé has as many as sixty-five key elements, divided among skills, style, proper relationship establishment, self-knowledge, ability to work through difficulties, and bringing closure to the relationship. In their book *The Elements of Mentoring*, Johnson and Ridley define mentorships as dynamic relationships within a profession. They write:

> Outstanding mentors are intentional about the mentor role. They select protégés carefully, invest significant time and energy in getting to know their protégés, and deliberately offer the career and support functions most useful for their protégés. Mentoring is an act of generativity—a process of bringing into existence and passing on professional legacy.[1]

There is, however, a dark side to mentoring. Because mentoring occurs within a profession, the statement, "Mentor knows best" carries a great deal of truth. The seasoned person really does know more about the training, experiences, and personal growth needed for success in the profession. Yet taken to the extreme, the protégé starts feeling like someone else's creation. With research clearly showing that both the mentor and mentee benefit in terms of career satisfaction and success, and longevity within organizations, far more is written about the sunny side of mentoring than the dark side of jealousies, demands on time, exploitation, overdependence, and overprotection.[2]

Avoiding the dark side requires nurturing independence, listening carefully to the mentee's hopes, dreams, and concerns, and ensuring that you are working yourself out of the job of mentoring. The goal is for your protégé to succeed *without* you. Leaders need to empower those they are leading, not make them overdependent.

Thus, while great mentors can be Extraverted or Introverted, and can prefer the Judging style of seeking closure or the Perceiving style of seeking options, research indicates the need for:

- Warmth
- Active listening skills
- Sincere, unconditional regard

- Respect for privacy, confidentiality
- Tolerance for admiration and idealizing
- Humor
- Acceptance of mistakes
- Integrity
- Empathy, understanding, and respecting values
- Lack of jealousy[3]

Further, mentors need to develop their own EQ before taking on someone else's development, and being selective about protégés is key. Consider the experiences of Tasha and Tyler.

Too Much Leading

Tasha was a manager at a large financial services firm. One of the aspects of her job that Tasha loved most was the chance to mentor the fresh-out-of-college women who reported to her. In some ways, they were carbon copies of herself fifteen years earlier. She had struggled for years without a mentor, though, and hadn't realized what a struggle that had been until a senior officer noticed a position paper she'd written and then tapped her for several special projects that were her ticket to promotion.

The young women on Tasha's team were being groomed for promotion far faster than she ever was, thanks to her mentoring efforts. They coauthored papers with her, learned how to give engaging presentations, attended meetings with senior management, and were sent to prestigious training programs.

One morning, her mentees gathered in her office as she explained a new opportunity. "The only way to learn how to lead is to lead," Tasha began. "This morning, the other managers and I agreed to have all the junior staff report to me, but the responsibility for supervising them will rotate among the three of you. You'll learn hands on about motivation, performance reviews, and even hiring practices and policies. Alexis, you'll go first since your undergraduate coursework included more management classes. Letting your coworkers take on your responsibilities for developing those training materials should free up time for these new responsibilities. Believe me! This will give each of you in turn a real edge for moving into roles in other departments."

Alexis looked a bit startled. She replied, "Give up the training materials? The training work interests me more than anything else I've tackled here. I was hoping to speak to you about how I might eventually take rotations at the corporate training center in New York."

Tasha shook her head impatiently. "Training is a dead end around here," she said. "Those forays to New York keep people from considering you for anything crucial. And crucial work is how you move up."

The Type/Emotional Quotient Connection

Tasha took an "I have your career all figured out" approach to mentoring. Not only had she failed to discuss career paths (other than following in her footsteps) with those she was mentoring, but she failed to consider her mentees, dreams, values, and priorities. Tasha's desire to help others showed in her commitment to mentoring. However, she needed to practice active listening skills in order to help her protégés identify opportunities that were right for them—instead of planning everything for them. Note that many, but certainly not all, leaders like Tasha who prefer both Extraversion and Thinking are more likely than leaders with other preferences to fall into this trap of organizing others instead of listening.

Listening in an empathetic way goes beyond knowing how people are feeling. Leaders also need to understand what causes those feelings and why certain events, emotions, or other factors cause others to react the way they do. Otherwise, mentors can easily slip toward unwittingly trying to clone themselves, or expecting mentees to conform to their wishes, or over-protecting them, or even becoming jealous.[4]

Still, having no plan for those you lead can be just as problematic.

Too Much Listening

Tyler, the head of a company's information technology department, firmly believed that people are different. He frequently commented, "Why on earth would you expect people to do things the same way? Even if you force compliance, why would you expect the same results?"

If members of his staff didn't want to upgrade their software packages, and had good reason, Tyler didn't force them. If they requested different work schedules, it was okay with him. While he of course required compliance with anything to do with corporate security, he often said that he cared about results, not rules. His team's impromptu staff meetings regularly centered around Tyler asking each person, "What do you need to better meet customer needs?" Legitimate creativity with his budget had allowed Tyler to handle most of their requests. His team produced work that was as good as or better than other divisions, so in his mind, he had no reason to manage his team differently.

However, Tyler's own manager, Ward, expressed growing concern over discrepancies among the departments. "It makes no sense to me," Ward began, "that your team ignores industry best practices. Any standardization we ask for is based on research, not whims. Your team can't dismiss research with 'I don't want to.'"

Tyler started to justify his policies with his team's track record, but Ward said, "You realize that no one from your team can be promoted outside of your department, or selected for any cross-team efforts, because they can't just jump in. They don't know the processes."

The Type/Emotional Quotient Connection

Whereas Tasha didn't listen enough, Tyler's listening skills were so strong that they got in the way of his understanding of the very real constraints of the organization. His personal biases blocked correct reading of the situation. Tyler valued empowerment so much that he lacked key insights regarding the environment in which his team operated. After the conversation with Ward, his team had to put in overtime to gain several competencies the company required.

Using the Leadership/Listening Lens

Leaders need to develop others, ensuring that they have the tools they need to do excellent work. However, without a focus on being intentional, it's too easy to let our own fears or disappointment with past experiences cloud our judgment. Tasha wouldn't have wanted her own mentor to dictate her future, but her zeal for helping younger women kept her from recognizing her misjudgment. Similarly, Tyler had seen great employees resign because of cookie-cutter work requirements. His emphasis on empowering his employees to make the most of their workplace blinded him to the fact that some corporate policies are indeed essential.

How might you falter as you foster employee development? In the following chart, highlight any leadership priorities that are on your top-ten list.

Leadership	Listening
Mentoring	*Empowering*
One of my major responsibilities as a leader is guiding or supporting others in identifying their goals and developing their potential.	I strive to enable others to learn to lead themselves and take initiative in their work.
Promoting	*Connecting*
I work to advocate for needed resources and "toot our horn" externally.	Listening to understand the viewpoints, feelings, and aspirations of those I lead increases my effectiveness.

Are you more like Tasha, or are you more like Tyler? Which of the following tasks resonate with you more?

- Do you envision employee career paths (like Tasha), or do you solicit employee dreams (like Tyler)?
- Do you increase employee visibility (like Tasha), or do you encourage employee initiatives (like Tyler)?
- Do you make suggestions (like Tasha) or listen for ideas (like Tyler)?

Considering these different tasks, where would you place yourself on the following scale—more like Tasha or more like Tyler?

Coaching Yourself as an Intentional Leader

Before considering the options for developing your skills for leading and listening, think about your goals:

- Will your mentoring efforts fall within the natural realm of your leadership role, or will you consciously seek more formal relationships with mentees outside of your team?
- Do you need to learn more about those you currently lead?
- Is listening a core area for growth?
- Are you too hands on or too hands off?
- Do you consciously think about your team's visibility and the role visibility can play in team members' career development?

Check your type page in the appendix (page 151) for learning strategies. Consider how you might alter any of the suggestions that follow to better meet your type. However, consider opportunities to stretch as well.

Options for Focusing on Mentoring

Check your mentoring skills. Look again at the list on pages 52–53 that identifies the key skills or attitudes that mentors need. Which skills do you perform well? Have you received feedback that indicates you might work to develop some skills?

Consider what it takes to become you. While coaching often involves skill development for current roles or future promotion, mentoring usually looks at career trajectories. Understanding how you got where you are today, including which experiences, skills, or knowledge were essential, is key to helping someone else succeed. However, with the speed of change in markets, technology, industries, and more, might younger professionals have different needs? Consider how others have gotten to where you are. Is your pathway still possible today, or have requirements and the competition changed? What knowledge can you pass on?

Know yourself. The type descriptions in the appendix (page 151) are set up so that the description of your type and the opposite type (for example, ISTJ and ENFP, where no preferences are shared) are on opposite pages. Read your own and then the opposite description. Consider the following questions:

- What natural inclinations for mentoring do I have?
- What values or priorities might others not share?
- What might I listen for to ensure I'm tuning into others' values rather than projecting my own?
- How might I irritate a mentee with different preferences? How might mentoring such a person be unproductive?
- What are my biases? How might I misinterpret someone who operates with a different yet equally legitimate values set?

Create an advocacy checklist. Sometimes, day-to-day demands are so crazy that we forget to think strategically or beyond the regular scope of responsibilities. At least once a month, work through this checklist. When have you:

- Sought opportunities for visibility for your team or mentees?
- Made sure that others knew of your team members' successes?
- Advocated for your team or mentees' developmental needs?

Learn to listen. Dr. Dario Nardi, while researching connections between type and brain activity, found that only two of the sixteen personality types regularly engage in intensive listening (ISFP and INFP). The rest of us either think about how we're going to reply or concentrate on our reaction to what is being said.[5] Fortunately, brain plasticity means we can learn to make better use of those regions that engage us more completely as listeners if we engage in deliberate practice.

People often benefit from a formal workshop on active listening or from practicing listening techniques frequently with a coach. You can start by developing a set of open-ended questions that will help you understand others' needs and aspirations. For example, ask:

- What would be most helpful to talk about today?
- Are you satisfied with the path you've taken to your current position? How? Are you dissatisfied? Why?
- If you could wave a magic wand, what career step would you take next?
- In what specific areas or skills are you seeking to improve or to gain experience?

- Where, or on what sort of endeavors, have you thrived in the past? Why did it work so well for you?

If their answers are short, resist the urge to fill in or start making suggestions. Instead, paraphrase and prompt with, "Tell me more" or "What else comes to mind?"

Options for Focusing on Listening

Empower instead of directing. The listening side of this lens helps leaders focus on helping employees learn to lead themselves. This involves coaching for employee development instead of managing for compliance. Thomas Crane has a checklist to help people consider whether they boss or coach. For example, do you:

- Direct and lecture others or facilitate their decision making?
- Come ready with answers or seek answers?
- Point out errors or encourage learning?
- Create structures and procedures or create a vision with flexibility?
- Focus on the bottom line or focus on processes that lead to the bottom line?[6]

Further, most managers need coaching on how to coach! If active listening skills and leaving tasks and questions open-ended are new to you, check whether your company offers any training. Books such as *Listening: The Forgotten Skill* (Burley-Allen) and *Switch: How to Change Things When Change Is Hard* (Heath and Heath) may also be helpful.

Make time. Connecting with people so that you understand why they engage in the work they do and what they hope to become takes time; it also can't be forced. No matter how busy your workplace, make sure you make space for casual sharing. At one office, we all lunched together on "food court Fridays." At another office, managers insisted that everyone take a few breaks together in the employee cafeteria during their busiest season. Several others create coffee and break stations within departments, decorated with signs such as, "Some of the Best Collaboration Happens Right Here." Another made a practice of inviting employees at various levels to lunch to discuss ways to improve the workplace.

Provide the what and why, not how. Be clear about the goals and expected results, but let employees figure out the hows themselves; this is a sure path to empowerment. Let employees prioritize timelines and decide how they will inform you of progress. Then, stay hands off unless they fail to follow through on keeping you apprised of progress. Be careful not to be impatient—especially if you are used to being hands on. Give people time to respond.

Wait for meetings. One of my most influential bosses left the details of most meetings up to his employees: how often, when, and what we'd discuss. He almost always made time for us within just a few hours of our request for a meeting. While topics were our responsibility, he asked to receive agendas or lists of our questions at the start of the meetings. His message was clear: he trusted that we could competently lead ourselves as well as judge when we needed his wisdom, advocacy, or approval. Try this open-invitation method instead of scheduling regular meetings.

Share the goal. Bill George, retired head of Medtronic, found when researching his book *True North* that most of the leaders he interviewed "had transformative experiences on their journeys that enabled them to recognize that leading was not about their success but the success they could create by empowering others to lead."[7] Can you think of a time when employees exceeded your expectations by going beyond what you asked them to do or imagined that they could do? Reflect on what motivated them. Identify other times that employees probably needed less instruction and more empowerment from you.

> Remember, the leadership/listening lens helps you navigate how to best develop others by guiding and by listening. How well do you balance your agenda with others' aspirations?

CHAPTER 6

Balancing Reality
With Vision

Lens 4

Sensing	Intuition
Reality	Vision
Loyalty, Accountability	*Visioning, Optimism*

What leader in his or her right mind would admit, "I don't really have a vision." At least not since the first President Bush was derided for saying, "Oh . . . the vision thing" when a friend suggested that he expand beyond his short-term goals. All of us want to know where our leaders intend to take us; inspiring with a shared vision is one of the top ten leadership tasks identified by Kouzes and Posner in *The Truth About Leadership.*

However, all of us *also* want to see visions that are grounded with realistic attention to constraints such as time, budget, and competing agendas within an organization. Leaders can aim high, but the vision needs to include a realistic picture of how to get there.

If you want the vision you're promoting to be meaningful, keep the following in mind:

- Organizational visions have little impact on employee commitment unless employees have identified their own personal beliefs and values and perceive that these fit with the company vision.[1]

- Successful companies define their visions in terms of who they are and their ongoing purpose rather than in terms of products and industries.[2] Medtronic, for example, has as part of its mission, "To contribute to human welfare." The Jim Henson Company's mission includes, "Making the world a better place by inspiring people to celebrate life." And who can miss the practicality of Reliable Courier & Delivery's vision? "On time, every time."

- Employees at all levels can provide significant insights toward the company vision. When I facilitate strategic planning, I involve people from all levels in setting the vision. Not only does the process incorporate the motivations of diverse workers, but it also increases awareness of how leadership decisions are formed. Whether leaders involve everyone in the process or instead gather ideas, the point is that visioning is most effective when it doesn't begin exclusively at the top.

Dee Hock, founder of Visa, says:

> Without a deeply held, commonly shared purpose that gives meaning to their lives; without deeply held, commonly shared, ethical values and beliefs about conduct in pursuit of purpose that all may trust and rely upon, communities steadily disintegrate, and organizations progressively become instruments of tyranny.[3]

A strong statement? Perhaps. But effective visions link the values or purposes that foster employee loyalty with the organization's forward-looking purposes. How does *why* people come to work fit with where the company is headed?

Leaders, though, sometimes espouse wonderful visions that border on wishful thinking, if not impossibility. For example, the owner of a small startup company I worked with had carefully crafted a vision of a web-based product and hired the best content experts, programmers, and marketing managers he could find. Did he have visionary goals? Yes. However, he created his vision without asking questions such as, "What might customers be willing to pay?" and "What are the competing products?" So while they were visionary, were the goals realistic? No, because his goals—and resulting product design—didn't match the realities of the market. His design got ahead of the facts.

Be wary, though, of considering the reality/vision lens only in intensive strategic planning processes. Let's visit two individuals who got out of balance in the general flow of work.

Too Much Reality

Karla managed a regulatory team at a multinational manufacturing firm. Her staff truly knew its stuff: staff members were masters of the state and federal regulations governing their products, concise communicators to other divisions concerning labeling requirements or product adjustment recommendations, and excellent wordsmiths.

All of them took pride in their tremendous attention to detail that following regulations required. They saw their work as serious and essential to the company, but were keenly aware that people in other departments considered them not just dull but ridiculously risk-averse. Occasionally their analyses sparked comments such as, "Here you go, raining on our parades again." Karla laughed off such remarks and told her team, "We aren't here to make other departments happy. And who cares if they like us! We're here to make sure things stay in compliance for the welfare of all."

Mark, a long-term employee, stopped her in the hall one day. "Marketing just emailed me that they won't add the additional labeling information and instructions we recommended for that new product," he said. "They say no one will buy it if the directions are that complicated. I really think it's the wrong call—what should we do?"

Karla sighed. "I'll resend your recommendation to my counterpart in marketing, but our job is to thoroughly inform them and then move on to the next project. I can't make them comply, especially since we know it's a grey area. Those recommended additions are only applicable in unusual circumstances."

Months later, though, Mark's wisdom was apparent as a host of consumer complaints led to a recall of the new product. Karla's boss, in a very unpleasant encounter for Karla, informed her of several other avenues for communicating her division's concerns that she could have pursued.

The Type/Emotional Quotient Connection

As a realist, Karla paid close attention to accountability. However, Karla hadn't defined it broadly enough, believing that her job ended when information left her department. Her Sensing preference, with no one guiding her to look beyond her department walls, had kept her from grasping how her team was foundational to the company's success. In EQ terms, Karla lacked a sense of social responsibility; her definition of product safety was bound up in regulations, not the actual impact on the health or safety of consumers. Key to EQ is seeing how one's efforts connect with a greater good. Developing this wider focus might have helped Karla realize the importance of being assertive in her interactions with other departments, another leadership skill she hadn't seen the need to cultivate. However, she was replaced shortly after the product recall. The new leader guided the team in helping other departments see how their work fit with the overall company vision of innovation, even if sometimes they had to say, "Slow things down. Listen for a moment. We're your best allies in avoiding another recall!"

Yet too strong a vision can also bring challenges.

Too Much Vision

Kent, head of a midsized manufacturing firm, had a wonderful problem—he'd landed a new client whose first order meant doubling their usual production output.

As a result, his shop had been running a third shift for several weeks; even Kent was taking turns on the graveyard shift. I suggested that his leadership team work through a structured analysis to get a better picture of this new client's impact on the firm. All but three of the twelve team members preferred Intuition, as did Kent; this process usually helps everyone find their voice on an issue.

I started the meeting by asking them to list the facts of the situation, the realm of the Sensing function. Filled with enthusiasm, Kent's team noted the lack of production delays. There hadn't been any breakdowns or excess wear on equipment in spite of 24/7 operation. Workers had welcomed the overtime pay and the fact that the officers were being paid at normal, not overtime rates, and so on. Even though I pressed for information on any emerging difficulties, a consensus quickly formed: the client was a boon for the company.

Our next step in the structured process involved Intuition and the possibilities this new client might open up for the company. Kent shared his plans for the increased revenue: technology upgrades, a more solid revenue base, the ability to compete for larger and larger companies, an enhanced worldwide presence, and more. His excitement increased as his top managers added to his ideas.

We then turned to the realm of the Thinking function to consider consequences, or possible downsides, of this sudden increase in needed capacity, such as vulnerability to machine breakdowns and possible effects on other customers. "The opportunities simply give us more ways to handle any such problems," Kent pointed out. "We can solve them with the increased resources."

Finally, we discussed the impact on people, the emphasis of the Feeling comments. The comments were at first all positive: "Morale is good, especially when Kent takes his shift." "People are excited that this customer might mean financial security." "The extra pay is great as we approach the end of the year." But then one person stood up, one of the three individuals who preferred Sensing, and said, "Back when we were discussing the facts, I couldn't get a word in. Here's one impact we didn't list: All of us are *human*. There's a real limit on this 24/7 business. Eventually that third-shift rotation is going to mess up health, families, relationships, or all three!"

The room went silent for a full minute. Then Kent gestured toward the possibility-filled charts on the walls of the meeting room and said, slowly, "You're right. Most of us are so enamored with our new future that we're ignoring the very real toll that our current course will take on the things we really care about."

The Type/Emotional Quotient Connection

Kent wasn't insensitive to others, but he hadn't consciously sought their opinions and concerns about his plans. Empathy would have helped ground his dreams in reality much sooner. Remember that our brains tend to filter out information that contradicts our positions or choices.[4] Checking our interpretations of events with those of other people keeps us aware of our biases so we can better judge the facts of a situation. In Kent's case, his vision of the future with this new customer included his desire to firmly establish his company as a player in the next tier of competitors, blinding him to any downside. Kent's vision had been strong enough to keep his employees motivated and excited about a future that was unfolding around them. In a very real sense, his leadership choices were exactly what the situation called for.

However, the meeting format ensured that Kent stepped back from his enthusiasm to consider whether the company's new plans were in step with employee values. With his preferences for Intuition and Thinking, Kent was easily carried away with strategic planning, forgetting the human element. The meeting forced him to use his Sensing (what is happening now, and what facts regarding the new customer are relevant to our decisions) and Feeling (the impact on people) sides.

In the end, after far more analysis, Kent's team modified their expansion plans to a three-phase approach that hinged on how many other larger customers they were able to procure.

Using the Reality/Vision Leadership Lens

This lens has a significant tie to your preferred way of gathering information. Those who prefer Sensing naturally pay more attention to reality, while those who prefer Intuition pay more attention to the future. Intentional leaders know their tendencies and explore ways of ensuring that they consider both.

What are your natural tendencies? Did your top ten leadership priorities include any of the priorities connected to the reality/vision leadership lens? If so, highlight them on the chart that follows.

Reality	Vision
Loyalty	*Visioning*
I thrive when my skills, experience, and motivations are a long-term match to individuals, organizations, or causes.	I believe in co-creating images of the future that motivate people and then leading them to work toward those common purposes.
Accountability	*Optimism*
I establish realistic expectations and responsibility for outcomes, striving for clarity regarding what is and isn't under our control.	I want to inspire confidence in those I lead that our efforts will bring success.

Which trap might be the bigger danger for you: Karla's too-narrow view of her department's importance or Kent's dilemma brought on by being too vision-oriented?

- Do you develop your team's skills and sense of importance (like Karla), or do you create a vision of your team's role in the larger organization (like Kent)?

- Do you set clear roles and responsibilities (like Karla), or do opportunities play a larger role in your focus (like Kent)?

- Do you set realistic expectations for success (like Karla), or do you want employees to shoot for the stars (like Kent)?

Consider these different options and rate where your focus lies on the following scale: are you more like Kent or more like Karla?

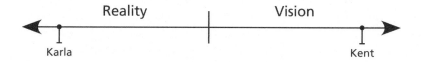

Coaching Yourself as an Intentional Leader

Before considering the options for improving your skills in using the reality/vision leadership lens, think through your starting place by identifying your goals. In working with this lens, are you striving for:

- A better understanding of why your team members come to work and what motivates them?

- Understanding whether or not others' reactions or opinions might help you unearth your own biases?

- Developing mutual understanding around accountability?

Which of the following common needs might be your best starting place for improving leading with vision?

- Understanding the beliefs and values of those you are leading

- Articulating your own beliefs

- Expanding the vision of the reach of your work

Check your type page in the appendix (page 151) for learning strategies. Consider how you might alter any of the suggestions in the following section to better meet your type. However, consider opportunities to stretch as well.

Options for Improving Your Focus on Reality

Think it through. Consider three recent endeavors that fell short of your expectations. Reflect on possible causes by responding to the questions in the following chart. Do you see any patterns?

Reflection Questions	Endeavor One	Endeavor Two	Endeavor Three
Was I unrealistic about the time the project would take?			
What information did I discount because of past experiences or my own enthusiasm?			
Did others share my vision? My reality? How do I know?			
What did I know about the motivations of others working on the project?			
What should I have done differently to reach my original goals?			

Check in. Does the vision you're espousing as a leader incorporate the values and beliefs of those that you're hoping the vision will guide? *Ask* the people you lead which skills they'd like to employ more, develop more, or use less. Find out if they know their own values and can relate them to the organization's mission. What information or results might help them understand how their work is carrying out the overall mission?

Find a critic. If you've received feedback that your plans are overly optimistic, consider who among your team members or peers might help you think through scenarios before you plan. Identifying and preparing for possible problems is a part of accountability. For example, in Kent's team meeting, his employees considered consequences of equipment breakdowns, changes in the customer base, and so on. Balancing optimism with a hard look at very possible disruptions to plans can increase trust and loyalty among employees.

Test your perceptions. After announcing a plan, facilitating a meeting, or otherwise interacting with your team, take some time to reflect. How do you think each person reacted? Then, ask about their reactions. Frame your questions so that you're more likely to get honest feedback. For example, ask, "I'm not sure I heard everyone's questions or concerns" or "This project is very important—I need everyone's honest take on the opportunities and barriers we face." Do your team members feel sufficiently informed? Are they optimistic? Enthusiastic? Frustrated? Overwhelmed? Do they feel heard? If you aren't sure they'll speak frankly, consider using a quick anonymous online survey through www.surveymonkey.com or a similar easy-to-use tool.

Assess your loyalty. Lifelong careers within one company are rare in today's economy. Further, the thought of remaining in the same environment feels stifling to people who also value variety. However, if many of the people you lead value loyalty, being able to articulate your sense of loyalty may help others understand you better. Think through your skills and talents and use them to fill in this blank: "As long as this organization values my ability to _____, I'd be interested in staying here." Or, come up with your own wording. You'll then be ready to speak to their values around loyalty by articulating how you contribute to the company and what you've received in return.

Options for Improving Your Focus on Vision

Reflect on your personal mission. Do you have a purpose, a cause, or something outside of your own needs or the specifics of your job that guides your decisions? In other words, are you clear on your own values and beliefs as a leader?

This is different from choosing your leadership priorities. For example, what if Karla's mission, what she hoped to accomplish, had been "Helping our company do what is best for consumers" instead of "Helping our company stay in compliance"?

Take the next step and construct a picture of yourself as a leader that is more than just your job description. From "Keeping my team cutting-edge" to "Developing my team into the most sought-after professionals in their fields (without losing them to recruiters)" to "Mentoring my replacements" to "Influencing others to model integrity," your mission should incorporate your own deep motivations.

Expand your vision. Is your vision for your team or organization big enough? Ask others what they expect from you and what your team would ideally accomplish if there were no constraints such as time or money. Yes, it may seem pointless to even ask such "what if?" questions, but they often spark ideas for new directions that still fit within the realm of reality. For example, what if Karla's vision had been, "Our efforts ensure that consumers know how to safely use every product."

Gauge your optimism. Optimism is another piece of emotional intelligence. Too little optimism not only blocks us from taking appropriate risks, but can lead to depression if everything seems to be out of our control. Consider three simple actions to increase your optimism:

1. Keep in regular contact with optimistic friends and coworkers.

2. Reflect on past times when you felt pessimistic. How often was it truly warranted? Often, people realize that they overestimate how often things turn out badly.

3. If your pessimism truly is warranted, consider meeting with a coach or counselor. What skill might you hone or what other proactive strategy, such as finding a way to alter your circumstances, might warrant new optimism?

Team on vision. Set aside at least three hours with your team to co-create a vision. Provide markers and large strips of paper (I cut flipchart paper into six to eight pieces) and meet in a room with lots of wall space. First, ask everyone to write down their vision for the department. Post all of them. Hold a discussion emphasizing the words people like, which ones capture ideas that the group hadn't considered, and other positive aspects of the posted visions.

Then, if your team has more than five people, split into groups of three to six and have each group compose a new vision, incorporating information from the individual visions and the discussion. Post all of these and again discuss which phrases resonate best with everyone. Often, at this stage, a final vision can be drafted, depending on the size of the group. If this is all very new to you, ask someone else to facilitate.

Stand up. It isn't enough just to have a vision; intentional leaders need to take a stand to see that vision becomes reality. If assertiveness isn't one of your strengths, consider meeting with a coach or mentor to reflect on how you can become more assertive. Identify past situations where you needed to be more assertive. Practice what you might have said in those situations. Then, do some planning for future situations.

> Remember, the reality/vision leadership lens helps you manage the tension between being grounded in what is and projecting optimism about what might be. Is the balance right—for different situations and for who you are as a leader?

CHAPTER 7

Balancing the Known
With the New

Lens 5

Sensing	Intuition
The Known	The New
Experience, Creativity with the known	*Challenge, Creativity with the new*

Few professions rely solely on what has worked in the past or what is working right now; even violin makers recently tapped MRI technology to better understand and imitate the techniques Stradivarius used to build the instrument. Yet limitless innovation has its problems, too. Once, after a two-day session on communication and problem-solving, I asked the head of a TV station to sum up what he learned. He told his leadership team and me that "We are fantastic at generating great, new ideas and challenges. We need to remember, though, that we are already doing great things that need to continue!"

Many leaders are generalists—they are always ready to take their ideas into new arenas. Delving more deeply into what is already working, however, requires specialists. Both generalists and specialists are valuable contributors in any workplace.

In the world of professionals, specialists and generalists follow very different pathways to success. Which one is more like you?

- *Specialists* work with what they know best, expanding their knowledge and expertise within a given domain. There's often a recognizable, although not set-in-stone, progression for building that expertise. From airline pilots to neurosurgeons to tax attorneys to electricians, these specialists begin their training with simpler versions of the complex tasks they aspire to master. Pilots don't start out flying 300-passenger jets; electricians don't start out developing wiring plans for skyscrapers. Their expertise develops as they tackle more and more complex endeavors. This deep expertise is priceless; if you're putting your brain in the hands of a neurosurgeon, you want to know that he or she has a deep, successful track record with heads, not feet.

- *Generalists* seek the new, expanding the arenas in which they use their skills. Maybe the best definition comes from the world of animals where generalist species are ones that thrive in a variety of habitats or adapt to several food sources. Leaders, writers, inventors, marketing and sales professionals, teachers, and consultants are just a few of the careers that lend themselves to generalists (although specialists can also find niches in all of these areas). I'm a generalist; although I've developed expertise in writing and Jungian type, I've used both in areas as diverse as spiritual retreats and math classrooms. Note that the Gallup *StrengthsFinder 2.0*[1] concentrates on the kinds of specialties that generalists transfer from one environment to another, a helpful framework for understanding effective ways to focus one's efforts.

Many generalists are motivated by the challenge of starting over on a brand-new playing field. Finding connections between past experiences and new situations, and applying creativity to excel at radically different problems and tasks holds more appeal than developing deep expertise in a defined role. This doesn't mean that generalists are "jack of all trades, master of none"; instead, they excel at bringing knowledge and insights to new situations, adding different points of view or needed expertise.

Many specialists are motivated to become the most experienced person in their current field. This doesn't mean that specialists stagnate; in fact, being the best usually means keeping tabs on new developments.

Neither path to excellence is better than the other. However, generalists can end up managing specialists, and specialists can end up managing generalists. These situations can result in effective synergy or complete misunderstanding. Intentional leaders know their own style, what their role calls for, and whether those they work with are most effective as generalists or specialists.

Consider the experiences of Ted and Tammi.

Stuck in the Known

Thoroughness was Ted's motto. Manager of a financial reporting compliance division, Ted knew that thoroughness was the key to monitoring the condition of the hundreds of firms his agency oversaw. Ted had worked his way up in his department, starting with the exhausting travel schedule of onsite audits, moving to reviewing reports as they came in, and then into leadership.

For the three years he'd been in charge, his team had easily met all of its deadlines and requirements. As his analysts worked through a set of reports, they filled out a summary sheet and then passed the whole report packet, with the summary, to him. Ted then used a technique of his own devising to review each summary, did random checks for accuracy, and prepared a detailed list of the results to pass on to his boss and, eventually, the board of directors.

The board of directors had recently acquired a new chairperson. After one monthly meeting, Ted's boss called him in to talk: "The new chair hates that summary report, Ted. Says it's meaningless—a 'smokescreen of ciphers' were his exact words. Of course, he didn't tell me what it is that he *does* want, just that you need to sit down with those new analysts in the special projects department and get their input."

Ted couldn't understand this. How could the chair not like his detailed work? How could he prefer a half-page report with a few statistics? Why would anyone willingly accept what those hotshot analysts produced? Apparently no one but Ted himself appreciated the power of his systematic monitoring.

The Type/Emotional Quotient Connection

Actually, I was one of the hotshot analysts, and Ted was right in thinking I didn't appreciate the number of times his perusal of every number had tipped him off to potential problems. I hadn't yet heard of personality type and lacked awareness of how my preference for Intuition caused me to discount Ted's need for documentation regarding how my condensed report still covered the necessary information. However, Ted, who probably preferred Sensing, didn't realize how our report accurately summarized the details in a useable form for the new chair who, with his generalist approach, could easily process the analysts' reports.

Ted was self-confident and rightfully proud of his deep expertise. However, his narrow focus had come at the expense of being flexible, another key component of EQ. Ted's situation had changed with the new chair, but he ignored evidence that his tried-and-true process wouldn't work anymore. In EQ terms, flexibility involves adjusting your thoughts, emotions, and behaviors to changing circumstances. Ted wasn't adept at longer-term strategizing and hadn't thought about helping his team's operations change as technology increased options for data gathering and analysis. The new board chair, with his varied background, knew there were better ways.

Change, though, requires considering what should be preserved as well as what needs to change. Here's an example of failing to understand the importance of experience.

Stuck in the New

I first heard from Tammi about six months after she started her new position as director of a nonprofit organization that specializes in counseling women in crisis. The organization chose her, an outsider, in part because of the huge grant they landed for next-step services. The organization, said Tammi, sought to "help after, not just during, crises so that women can get the support they need to change their lives. Abuse, difficulties in parenting, job retention . . . there are so many needs."

Tammi then summarized why she had called me: "I inherited a staff that sees our chance to design new programs as an affliction, not a fantastic opportunity to make a lasting difference to our clients. I keep emphasizing, 'We get to start from scratch, designing while keeping in mind the resources of this town and the patterns of need in the women we serve.' And they look at me like I'm an alien. 'Can't we borrow from other agencies?' they ask. Or they say, 'Clients want a fresh start. They won't want to return here—to the place they fled to on the worst night in their lives.' Those are all just excuses to avoid working on the program designs, I'm sure. They're lazy!"

In conflict situations, I need to hear everyone's perspectives, not just the leader's. In interviewing the crisis counselors at Tammi's organization, I got a very different picture of why they hadn't dived into designing the new program.

One counselor explained, "What I'm best at is listening—facilitating the client's thoughts regarding what to do next. Tammi doesn't get that I don't plan. Counseling is the antithesis of planning."

Another commented, "Tammi gives no direction other than 'Make it so.' A real leader would give us parameters, information, models—in short, would lead!"

Another counselor noted, "I lack experience in every area she's asking me to design. We need outside expertise at this stage."

After reading the anonymous feedback, Tammi said, "Is this accurate? I'm saying they have freedom to design whatever they believe is best, and they want me to tell them exactly what to do?"

The Type/Emotional Quotient Connection

Generalists and specialists often have these kinds of clashes when change is called for. Tammi was highly self-aware and comfortable with new and ambiguous efforts. With her preference for Intuition, she loved being self-directed, and she assumed that her team would crave challenges and innovation as much as she did. Her strong sense of independence actually blocked her ability to empathize, problem-solve, and direct her new team.

Using the Known/New Leadership Lens

A key factor for the known/new leadership lens is the level of comfort people have when pursuing options, tasks, careers, experiences, or situations with which they have no direct experience. Especially early on in their careers, many Sensing types (like Ted and most of Tammi's staff) say, "Being asked to do something I haven't specifically trained for is like stepping into a black hole. How can I possibly know for sure what to do?" In contrast, many Intuitive types (like the hotshot analysts and Tammi) say, "How exciting to be asked to do something so novel. Think of all I'll learn along the way—I can picture the results!"

What are your natural tendencies? Were any of your top ten leadership priorities connected with the known/new leadership lens? If any of the following priorities seem unimportant, even if you were in a different leadership role, you might want to take a hard look at what that side of the lens has to offer.

The Known (Specialist)	The New (Generalist)
Experience	*Challenge*
I thrive when our knowledge and past work are key to improving performance or to planning and implementing new but related work.	I'm motivated by exciting problems or difficult, risk-filled tasks that enhance skills and prove competency.
Creativity with the known	*Creativity with the new*
I value using sound judgment, proven routines, and known information for continuous improvement in practical matters.	I value using my imagination and inspirations to devise original ideas, theories, tools, methods, or plans that bring about change.

Are you more likely to fall into the specialist leadership traps like Ted or the generalist traps like Tammi?

- Do you prefer being promoted from within (like Ted), or do you like increasing responsibility by changing organizations (like Tammi)?

- Do you set a clear path to expectations (like Ted), or do you prefer to set the goal and let ways to meet it emerge (like Tammi)?

- Do you improve what works (like Ted), or do you innovate to break new ground (like Tammi)?

Considering these different options, where would you place yourself on the following scale—more like Ted or more like Tammi?

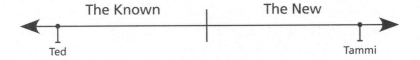

Coaching Yourself as an Intentional Leader

Before developing your ability to use the known/new leadership lens, take the following steps:

- Identify your goals. Are you trying to change yourself, those who work for you, or your ideas about what to keep and what to change? Are you adept at understanding the needs of generalists, those who love to build on experience, versus specialists, those who love to launch into the unknown? How might you misinterpret the actions of others within these areas?

- Check your type page in the appendix (page 151) for learning strategies. Consider how you might alter any of the suggestions that follow in the next section to better meet your type. However, consider opportunities to stretch as well.

Options for Improving Your Focus on the Known

Study the experts. If you are leading specialists, be sure you understand how they develop their expertise. Also, ask for recommendations for areas you might study deeply. For example, when I was a member of the board of directors of my professional association, we were all quite impressed when our new managing director asked to take a significant training course in the theoretical framework we all used so that he would have a better understanding of our work.

Analyze what's been done. Often, people with a preference for Intuition enjoy creating far more than reusing. One team I worked with that was made up completely of intuitive members posted a sign during their planning meetings to help them focus on the known. It read, "What's worked before? What's been done? Where should we not reinvent?"

Ask, "Why are we doing it this way?" Work to see the value in routines others have created. Study how given procedures save time or help workers avoid mistakes. For example, back in my "hotshot analyst" days, I picked up several tips from a great discussion with Ted about his process for double-checking the summary report and revised our new format to make use of some of his calculations.

Relate to the hedgehog. Recall Collins's hedgehog concept presented in *Good to Great*. While foxes have many tricks, hedgehogs have just one defense: rolling into a ball. Whereas foxes can take a scattered approach, hedgehogs:

> Simplify a complex world into a single organizing idea, the basic principle or concept that unifies and guides everything. It doesn't matter how complex the world, hedgehog reduces all challenges and dilemmas to simple—indeed almost simplistic—hedgehog ideas. Anything that does not somehow relate to the hedgehog idea holds no relevance.[2]

What is your hedgehog? If you can be more specific about the qualities or skills you bring to leadership, such as troubleshooting before a planning flaw causes problems, or supporting strategies that involve some risk, it might make it easier for the specialists you lead to relate to how you operate.

Motivate change. If you are working to help yourself or others develop deeper expertise or the processes and routines that help you avoid mistakes, check out the framework for change described in *Switch: How to Change Things When Change Is Hard* by Chip and Dan Heath. Using the framework of defining why change is necessary ("direct the rider"), engaging your emotions as well as your mind ("motivate the elephant"), and making it easier to go in the right direction ("shape the path"), the authors present nine overall strategies and dozens of examples on how to make the strategies they suggest work for you.[3]

For example, motivate the elephant to follow procedures by making a list of times when ignoring procedures created problems. Direct the rider to identify your hedgehog strength or framework by identifying exactly how someone you admire has been rewarded because of his or her hedgehog.

Options for Improving Your Focus on the New

Learn strategy. Read the *Harvard Business Review* and *Businessweek,* keeping a lookout for case studies on strategizing. Ask yourself, "How does this case study relate to my field of work? What connections can I make? What new insights do those give me?" Consider reading Ram Charan's book *What the CEO Wants You to Know: Using Business Acumen to Understand How Your Company Really Works.* Meet with others in your department who don't think like you, and work together to identify changes in customers, technology, the competition, and so on.

Identify your generalist side. Pick up a copy of *StrengthsFinder 2.0*[4] and work through the online survey. Identify core strengths you have that could be put to use outside of your department. Concentrate on those transferable skills (such as Achiever, Includer, Learner, and Strategic skills) that tie to leadership rather than to your particular profession.

Change a process or routine. Choose one to five routines or procedures that you or your team use regularly and analyze them by asking the following questions:

- What glitches have occurred when we use this process or routine?
- What changes to our work, technology, or personnel have been made since this procedure was finalized?
- Where is this routine most vulnerable to error? To outside pressures or mistakes? To other problems?

Select at least one of the routines or processes and change it, using your answers to guide your work.

Embrace your creativity. In *Orbiting the Giant Hairball*,[5] Gordon MacKenzie points out that if you ask first graders which of them are artists, every hand goes up. If you ask second graders, about half the hands go up. By sixth grade, nearly every hand stays down. When pressured to be "normal," we deny our creative edge, even though all of us have one.

If you are more comfortable with the known, keep in mind that the majority of innovation comes from building on existing products and processes; even the newest tablet computers are improvements to smartphones rather than an entirely new invention. Embrace your ability to create via your thorough knowledge of how things work best, all the time striving to see how the environment is changing and how new ideas might connect with what you know.

Motivate yourself. Check out the framework for change described in *Switch: How to Change Things When Change Is Hard* by Chip and Dan Heath. Use the authors' framework of defining why change is necessary ("direct the rider"), engaging your emotions as well as your mind ("motivate the elephant"), and making it easier to go in the right direction ("shape the path") and their nine strategies and numerous suggestions to help strengthen your motivation.[6]

For example, if you choose to read *Harvard Business Review* as one of your top ways of improving your strategic skills, you might shape the path by arranging a weekly breakfast with a colleague to discuss articles. Or, to better employ your generalist side, you might motivate the elephant by identifying a few small steps you could take, such as volunteering to help out at a community event that would use one of your strengths.

> Remember, the known/the new leadership lens helps you manage the tension between specializing and honoring current success and generalizing and carrying that success into new realms. Are the known and the new in balance for your current situation?

CHAPTER 8

Balancing Clarity With Ambiguity

Lens 6

Sensing	Intuition
Clarity	Ambiguity
Efficiency, Dependability	*Openness, Originality*

Some workplaces thrive because workers constantly ask, "Why are we doing it this way? Can we change?" Other workplaces thrive when workers *seldom* ask that question and instead carefully follow clear and specific procedures, changing them only after following a procedure for doing so.

Problems arise when we're too clear *or* too ambiguous with processes for a given situation. Here's an example. Quick—solve this problem in your head:

$$16 \times 35 = \underline{\hspace{2cm}}$$

If your mind immediately tried to activate the standard process (*algorithm* in math speak) for multiplication, you may still be trying to carry the three and remember several sets of digits. But if you instead thought about it differently, remembering that $8 \times 2 = 16$ and that multiplication is commutative, then you were quickly able to compute $8 \times 70 = 560$. Procedures can be wonderful, but they can also block exploration of better ways.

Rushing toward goals, we often don't consider whether we're doing things right or even doing the right thing in the first place. In many instances, procedures have been thoroughly vetted and are truly the best way (for example, using the standard algorithm to calculate 176 × 83).

Sometimes, procedures let us stop thinking, and it's okay.

Other times, we need to think. Push the envelope. Think outside the box. Clichés, yes, but clichés that caught on quickly because all too often situations beg for the wisdom those phrases convey.

Usually, work environments favor one end of this spectrum—clarity or ambiguity—over the other. Manufacturing firms frequently favor efficiency and dependguity). Research labs need both. What about your environment?

Intentional leaders explore how their areas of responsibility benefit from each side of the clarity/ambiguity lens. For example, if you ran a transit agency, would you solicit ideas from workers or expect them to follow procedures? Miam-Dade Transit listens to everyone. They expect employees to think about how procedures might be improved even as they follow them, and they pay employees who have improvement ideas that work. Observant employees such as maintenance technician Morris Penrod, who has generated over eighty money-saving tips himself, have received thousands of dollars over the years under this program.[1]

However, seeking out new ideas and allowing individual expression take time and (sometimes) come at the expense of efficiency, resulting in tension. Consider the following chart.

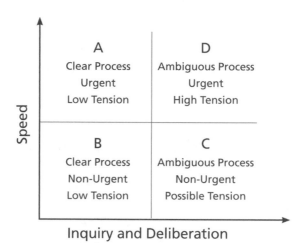

There is little tension in quadrant A. Urgency has everyone wanting to move quickly, and the path is clear.

Usually, quadrant B also produces little tension. However, it harbors the danger of complacency, the "We've always done it this way" syndrome.

Quadrant C is heaven for those who want to put their own stamp on things, but it can cause tension when others who value clarity think it's time to wrap up and move on.

Tension is highest in quadrant D, when the way forward is ambiguous and time is of the essence.

Different regions of our brain take over decision processes when we have different time frames. When we sense urgency, our survival instincts activate the amygdala, the area of the brain that triggers emotions. Not only do our emotions play a bigger role, but our ability to see various options decreases. The prefrontal cortex, usually active in choosing among options while keeping the long-term, big picture in mind, can be hijacked by emotions under stress, leading to poor decision-making.[2]

Understanding which quadrant you favor, and the natural tensions among the quadrants your position inherently incorporates, can help you appropriately manage the trade-offs between speed and thorough inquiry.

Let's look at two leaders who struggled to manage this lens.

Too Much Clarity

Six at a time, I interviewed all the employees at a distribution center for a large manufacturer. The company knew workers were particularly unhappy and that employee turnover interfered with efficiency. However as Ashley, the day shift manager, put it, "They aren't paid to be happy, but to be on time, follow directions, and work quickly. They receive bonus pay as long as they reach quota. I'm curious as to what they say, but this is work, not a beach party."

I discovered that employees were struggling to find any source of motivation. In many ways, they expressed that "None of us are working here because we want to. They might as well post a sign saying, 'Check your brains at the door.'" They described the mind-numbing nature of the work—reading orders, following packing charts, lifting, unloading, and the unrelenting updates on the sign tracking whether the shift was on schedule.

When we met to discuss the employee comments, I suggested to Ashley that we hold a planning session to consider other ways of organizing work. "They all feel like robots," I explained. "Maybe there's a way to resequence tasks, change configurations, or add some two-person elements that would maintain efficiency, yet better engage employees."

Ashley shook her head. "We had experts design the floor. It's the best it can be."

Only lengthy discussion regarding the true costs of the employee turnover rate—including the time she put into reviewing applications, interviews, and training, as well as absenteeism rates—changed her mind. Employees did in fact generate several great ways to improve their environment when she held a meeting for that purpose.

The Type/Emotional Quotient Connections

Ashley preferred Sensing and Thinking, which made it easy for her to value the company's current definitions of efficiency and success; she was being measured by the efficiency of her team. However, her approach didn't make room for the truth about what motivates people: autonomy, mastery, and purpose.[3] Only one worker out of the dozens I interviewed had found purpose in his work by envisioning customer satisfaction with correctly filled orders. Ashley fell into quadrant B on the chart; she saw a clear process, urgency, and low tension. She saw no reason to reorganize how the work was done.

Ashley's unwillingness to gather input from employees, and her belief that the current processes were the only pathways to efficiency, kept her from grasping how the very real employee turnover rates also affected efficiency. She needed to think beyond bonus pay to address turnover, using empathy in speaking with employees to understand what might and might not work.

While Ashley needed to place a higher value on being open to new perspectives and unique solutions, as always, these qualities can also be overemphasized.

Too Much Ambiguity

Aaron was the new head of the board of his professional association, which was made up of volunteers elected from the membership. Once a year, they gathered face-to-face to update the strategic plan and brainstorm how to support each other in meeting each goal.

The meeting also marked the formal handing over of the board presidency role. To kick off the day-long meeting, the past president took a few moments to congratulate everyone on progress the previous year. He announced, "Two of the biggest goals of course carry over—marketing the high-impact event we've been planning for months, and really ramping up our social network presence, now that we finally have a decent web platform. I'd suggest taking a chunk of today to write copy, contact potential partners, identify blog topics and authors, and make sure we all know how to use the new technology."

Aaron nodded in agreement with the past president and then launched into his agenda. "We'll start with a fresh look at where we need to be five years from now. Everyone, use the three sheets of paper in front of you to record your three top wishes for your areas of responsibility, one per sheet. We'll be posting these around the room."

Energy was so high during the activity that Aaron kept it going all morning. As lunchtime approached, the past president suggested that Aaron divide the group into a marketing subgroup and a social media subgroup to address the two main goals he identified that morning. The groups could brainstorm ideas while they ate. Aaron dismissed the idea, saying that the group needed a full break. By the time they finished the three wishes activity that afternoon, they barely had time for their formal, required business meeting before they hurried off to catch their flights.

Consequently, the new marketing director received no help in developing the important event marketing plan, spending weeks struggling on his own. In addition, only he and the past president were active in the social media channels.

The Type/Emotional Quotient Connections

Aaron's style falls into quadrant C. He completely missed that the marketing and social media goals needed attention; they were urgent, but there was as yet no clear plan for tackling them, placing them squarely in quadrant D. In his enthusiasm, Aaron failed to see the very real need for spending time on activities that related directly to revenue generation. He didn't realize that his own intuitive curiosity about unexplored possibilities and his desire to give board members the chance to make their own marks and follow their interests blinded him to the limits on their time. Yes, volunteer board members usually have vast needs for autonomy, but intentional leaders manage the tension between what could be done and what absolutely must be done.

Roger Pearman describes several different components of interpersonal EQ, including *energy*, which he defines as commitment toward including others and the ability to lead while being appropriately assertive and task-oriented. While Aaron related well to everyone, he needed to develop this leadership quality of *energy*.[4]

Using the Clarity/Ambiguity Leadership Lens

Ashley was right to emphasize clarity: manufacturing calls for procedures and efficiency. And Aaron needed to tap the wisdom of every board member; volunteers, after all, "unvolunteer" if they are dissatisfied. But both Ashley and Aaron were too comfortable with their methods, which blinded them to the insight they could acquire from the other side of this lens.

Those with a preference for Sensing are often pulled toward the clarity side of this lens, and those who prefer Intuition toward the ambiguity side. What are your natural tendencies? Did your top ten leadership priorities include any of those connected with the clarity/ambiguity leadership lens? Highlight any priorities from your list that appear on the chart that follows.

Clarity	Ambiguity
Efficiency	*Openness*
I want to organize our work environments, processes, tasks, and so on, so that goals are met with little waste of time, talent, or materials.	I seek and ponder contrary data, new perspectives, and other points of view before reaching conclusions.
Dependability	*Originality*
I want to be known as trustworthy and reliable, carrying out the responsibilities I have been given.	I value tapping our imaginations, and connecting ideas in unusual ways, and using artistic skills or other tools to find unique pathways.

There is a place for precise documentation, set procedures, and well-vetted policies based on clear data, facts, and past experience. People with a preference for Sensing often value these things. There is also a place for leaping into the unknown, which is often easier for people who prefer Intuition. Which way do you lean?

- Do you prefer the tried and true (like Ashley), or do you seek new ideas and approaches (like Aaron)?

- Do you seek proven expertise (like Ashley), or do you seek new voices (like Aaron)?

- Do you ensure reliability (like Ashley), or do you allow uniqueness (like Aaron)?

Considering these different approaches, where would you place yourself on the following scale—more like Ashley or more like Aaron?

Coaching Yourself as an Intentional Leader

Before developing your ability to use the clarity/ambiguity leadership lens, consider the following questions:

- Which end of the spectrum is most important in your current role? Think about the quadrants described in the chart on page 80. How much might your future roles require the other side of the lens?

- What are your development goals?
  - Where might you benefit from a bit more clarity or standardization?
  - Where might leaving things open be helpful?

- Are you in tension with your employer or those you lead over this lens?

Check your type page in the appendix (page 151). How might you adjust the development options you choose to better meet your learning style? As always, consider options that might present a good opportunity to stretch.

Options for Improving Your Focus on Clarity

Read. Have you read your job description recently? What about your strategic plan? How about your company's key policies and procedures? Take some time to sit down with these documents. Mark with a highlighter or sticky notes:

- Things that surprise you
- Areas you overlook or underemphasize
- Practices and procedures you sidestep in ways that probably cause difficulties

Look for patterns. When does your natural creativity or your need for options provide less than optimal results?

Check your timing. Time often seems infinite for people who prefer ambiguity; there is always time to improve something further or hear voices that have not yet been heard. Consider a time when others hinted that an issue didn't warrant the time you invested or a decision was delayed, leading to problems for others. Was anyone questioning your timing, mentioning deadlines, or pushing for closure so that he or she could continue with other responsibilities? How might you recognize when enough is enough?

Consult your opposite. One of my colleagues is a master at finding new voices to inform our work. She relies on me, though, to determine the last possible moment for gathering input if we are to still make a deadline—and for recalling information we've gathered in the past. Understanding each other's strengths and needs makes this a successful alliance. Who might provide some balance for you in using this lens?

Experience the existing process. Choose one existing procedure, task, plan, or protocol and do it exactly as scripted. As you do so, pay attention to how and why it works. What wisdom went into creating it?

Ponder the cost of efficiency. Sometimes, our drive for efficiency truly gets in the way of wisdom. Margaret Wheatley points out that when we choose to measure one thing, or to experiment in one way, we close off other possibilities. We're constructing which world we will know. She comments:

> For leaders, being alert to the observation dilemma is critically important.
> Management is addicted to numbers, taking frequent pulses of the organization

in surveys, monthly progress checks, quarterly reports, yearly evaluations. It is important to stay aware to the realization that no form of measurement is neutral. Every act of measurement loses more information than it gains. So how can we ensure that we obtain sound information to make intelligent decisions? How can we know what is the right information to look for? How can we remain open to the information we lost when we went looking for the information we got?[5]

Her recommendations for minimizing the harmful effects of the observation dilemma very much tap the wisdom of the ambiguity side of this lens: gathering more participants who own the plan generated by the information, adding subjective data, examining actual relationships while looking past official hierarchies, and searching for actual reactions, catalysts, and impacts.

Take a hard look at one tool you are using to measure efficiency or dependability. What other data might you consider? What other questions might you examine with other data sources? What might you be missing?

Options for Improving Your Focus on Ambiguity

Ask two more people. Even if you think you know all you need to know about a situation, check with at least two more people. Ask them what other questions they might raise, what other data they might examine, or what similar situations they've dealt with. Use their answers to consider what your own blind spots might be.

Ignore your standard operating procedures in small ways. Consider taking a different route to work. Compose a document without looking at a previous template or example. Add a bit of artistry, whether it's extra colors on a flipchart or taking the time to articulate a clever analogy that helps to explain a decision or a variety of perspectives.

Find your devil's advocate. Who thinks differently from you? Whose questions sometimes make you cringe because you know you should have thought to raise them yourself? Who is your best devil's advocate? Find a way to incorporate that person's input into your decisions.

I have a list of colleagues who fill this role for me. Whenever I'm starting a new project, I choose a few of them, write up my favorite ideas, and correspond via email or meet with them to find out what they think.

Ask, "What if?" In *Scenarios: The Art of Strategic Conversation,* Kees van der Heijden describes his methods for looking at various possible scenarios (futures) based on uncertainties that companies face. Explore his in-depth methodology for choosing key business concerns, developing different stories about the future depending on which possibilities become reality, and then embedding those what-ifs in your team's psyche. Your team is then better prepared to see how the environment might be changing. He writes:

> The language of scenarios is about the future, but they should make a difference in what is happening now. If it is successful in embedding different models of the business environment in the consciousness of the organization, it will make the organization more aware of environmental change. Through early conceptualization and effective internal communication, scenario planning can make the organization a more skillful observer of its business environment. By seeing change earlier the organization has the potential to become more responsive. Its decisions will also become more robust; there will be less "I should have known that."[6]

You can't avoid all possible scenarios, but you can assess the possibilities and consider ways to lessen the impact. For example, what would happen if a key employee fell ill or left? What if laws or regulations change? What breakthrough would you love to see, and what if a competitor gets to it first? How might a market shock or threat to national security affect your plans? What else could happen? Ask these questions, and more, and consider what you need to do to weather these kinds of events.

Incorporate originality. Consider where you can turn employees loose. In what situations could you say, "As long as we get the desired outcome, you may complete this project any way you wish"? For example, a team to which I once belonged was given the task of creating a training program about new financial instruments that would heighten awareness of the risks involved. Allowed to create anything we wanted, we came up with a presentation that used a set of case studies rather than a straightforward informational format. The freedom sparked our creativity, and the results were so well received that we ended up repeating the program many times.

The drive that many people have to put their unique stamp on things is often astounding to those who seek the most expedient path. Consider the values of the personality type opposite your own in the appendix (page 151; opposite types are printed on adjacent pages). Can you see how you and your opposite type differ with this lens?

> Remember, the clarity/ambiguity lens helps you manage the tension between standardization and openness to new processes and ideas. As you lead, are you striking the right balance for your current situation?

CHAPTER 9

Balancing Logic and Values

Lens 7

Thinking	Feeling
Logic	Values
Fair-mindedness	*Empathy*

We all want leaders who make good decisions. And, as leaders, we certainly want to be known as good decision makers. But what makes a good decision?

Logical objectivity—considering if/then, pros/cons, and causes/effects—is often held up as best practice in making sound choices. If your first thought is, "Well of course. We need to be rational," consider this: you can be rational without being logical.

As summarized on pages 21 and 22, type theory shows how the Thinking way of making decisions, which is a *logic*-driven decision-making process, and the Feeling way of making decisions, which is a *values*-driven decision-making process, are both rational. If there is any doubt, consider the research.

In *How We Decide*, Jonah Lehrer draws on a wide range of research to show that we do not, and should not, rely on logic to make many decisions.[1] For example, researchers gave ten dollars to one subject and asked the subject to divide it with another by making an offer. The second subject could accept the offer, resulting in each person keeping their portion of the proposed split, or refuse it, leaving both parties empty-handed. The researchers thought people would behave logically, making and accepting low offers. After all, the second subject should be happy with one dollar rather than nothing. However, the average offer was around five dollars each—a fair split. Why? Because people use not just logic but empathy when making decisions. We treat others how we'd like to be treated; subjects offered the amount of money they themselves wanted to receive.

The values-driven decision to offer five dollars may not have been logical (it meant less money to the person who offered), but it was rational. Why? Because if you base decisions only on logic when people are involved, actual results may differ significantly from the predicted results. This may seem obvious, but leaders make this error all the time.

Lehrer also reported that one little change in this experiment caused people to behave more logically: when the person making the offer wasn't in the same room as the responder. Then the offers matched what was predicted: they were lowball offers. Think about the implications. How often do leaders make decisions in the absence of those who will be affected? For example, what if decisions about potential layoffs were made with those who were about to be pink-slipped in the same room as the decision makers? Would leaders be more likely to at least consider decreasing their own compensation and sharing before enacting layoffs?

To add a second piece of research to the value of using both logic and empathy, Dario Nardi found that people with different type preferences differed in the amount of brain activity in the areas of the neocortex associated with objective reasoning and values-driven reasoning. While education, practice, and culture can all assist us in using more areas of our brain, there's evidence that, based on our type preferences, we're predisposed to first consider either logical or values-driven criteria.[2]

The answer to the question "What makes a good decision?" then, isn't as straightforward as it may seem: sometimes logic leads to better decisions, and at other times, the better decisions are driven by values. Nevertheless, a few key actions seem to be involved in making good decisions:

- Make sure you're solving the right problem. In the stories that follow, you'll see how incorrectly defining a problem or its root causes can lead to erroneous approaches to solving it.

- Choose appropriate criteria. The relevant importance of emotions and logic depend on the situation. For example, when buying a house, criteria such as cost per square foot fade from memory during the day-to-day experience of satisfaction with the floor plan, décor, views, or neighborhood. On the other hand, only logic may be needed to choose between two short-term rental properties.

- Consider your own mental strengths: do you excel in logic or empathy? How often do you overlook the options this lens helps you explore?

So what do decisions look like when we get too far out of balance—depending either too much on logic or too much on empathy and other human-centered values?

Too Much Logical Objectivity

Back in the 1980s, Minneapolis was hit with an ice storm just before morning rush hour. For the first time in fifty years, the transit commission pulled all public buses from the road. Many businesses declared a snow day, giving employees the day off with pay. Then, just a few weeks later, it happened again. For a lot of companies, providing that second snow day was problematic. I happened to be in a meeting the morning after the second storm with several senior managers. One manager, Elaine, stated, "I don't see why we should give another day with pay. People can just take a vacation day. That's what I do when my children get sick or I need to paint my grandmother's house or the roads are bad. Vacation days are the answer."

I said, "But you have five weeks of vacation. Eighty percent of the employees here only get two weeks, and they have to take an entire week at once for audit purposes. With only five extra days, think how they'd resent losing one—or more—to a snow day."

She looked at me for a full five seconds before saying, "I never thought of that."

A few weeks later, management agreed on a snow day rule: If the buses are running, get to work or take a vacation day. If they aren't, stay home with pay. Essential personnel need to plan in advance to ride with someone who has all-wheel drive. Simple, easy to implement (bus cancellations are announced via television, Internet, and radio), and fair to the business as well as employees.

In the world of business, objectivity and impact on the bottom line usually rule. After all, picture the chaos if businesses made different rules about snow days for every employee: cries of "Not fair!" would echo through the buildings. However, by not stepping into the shoes of those involved, Elaine almost created an unfair policy, albeit unintentionally.

The Type/Emotional Quotient Connection

Elaine, an attorney, was well trained in logical reasoning. She also preferred Thinking. While these factors drove her initial reaction, she accepted my reasoning immediately. She soon added with a laugh, "If the buses aren't running, forcing people to drive on the worst roads ever or else lose pay is probably a really bad idea." She had a new definition of the problem. Rather than just thinking of the effect of extra vacation days on the company's bottom line, she reframed it as, "What rule would be objective, consider employee safety, and be fiscally responsible?" This incident helped her understand the importance of interpersonal EQ skills, a good balance for her Thinking values for logic and objectivity.

This example is relatively straightforward, but the impact on people is routinely left out of the equation in many companies when they consider policies, processes, cost-saving measures, and so many other areas that lend themselves to quantitative or logical analysis. One of the worst situations I've seen in terms of human wreckage was the logical decision to pit two equally competent managers against each other; whoever "won" in terms of productivity would be the next department head when the current one retired at the end of the year. The competition of course destroyed trust throughout the department. No one had considered the human cost of the contest.

However, leading with too much empathy can cause equally problematic results.

Too Much Empathy

A nonprofit organization hired me to run a full day of teambuilding with its entire staff and then meet with each of the six departments individually to set collaboration goals. During the contracting process, I quizzed Evan, the executive director, on the quality of relationships and the reasons for having me work with his organization. "Oh, everything is going fine," he repeatedly told me. "I schedule these yearly gatherings to ensure that we know each other as individuals. We get so busy serving our needy clients that we forget to even say hello to each other! That's why I want you to help each team choose a goal and then guide them in setting realistic action steps. Working together at least some of the time will then be embedded in their jobs."

The entire staff gave high ratings to the teambuilding day. The team meetings were fun and productive—except one. The community relations team had emailed me ahead of the training. "We just need a little brush-up on our communication skills," they said. "We've worked so little together recently." I suggested we start with one of my safest, most tried-and-true exercises. The three women each brought to the meeting:

- A list of their contributions to the team
- Their completion of the statement, "To do my best work as part of this team, I need _____."
- A commitment they were making to improve their collaborative skills

Every *other* time I've used this exercise, participants add to their teammates' lists of contributions and together craft strategies for improving teamwork. But this time, after the first person finished reading her contributions, and the second person affirmed them, the third team member said, calmly and coldly, "I will never have anything nice to say to you as long as I live."

After I picked the pieces of the meeting up off the floor (and I don't remember exactly how I did that), I confronted Evan with the summary. "One of your teams has deep, deep issues," I said. He bit his lower lip, squeezed his hands together, and said, "Oh . . . community relations? I had so hoped that their problems had blown over."

This surprised me almost as much as the disastrous team meeting. I replied, "You knew they pretty much hate each other and you didn't tell me? I asked you all those questions as we were designing sessions to avoid these kinds of problems. Conflict requires a whole different approach!"

The Type/Emotional Quotient Connection

Evan's preferences were for Feeling, which does correlate with higher EQ skills, such as empathy. However, in this case his empathy with each member of the recalcitrant team had blinded him to the real consequences of conflict. As I worked with the team, I quickly discovered how their infighting had spilled into other departments. With "harmony at all costs" as his top criteria for decisions, Evan hadn't come to terms with how this stance furthered disharmony. In addition, he tended to be more accommodating than assertive. He admitted that he hated dealing with conflict and had therefore done little with this team other than encourage them to bury their differences.

Using the Logic/Values Leadership Lens

Businesses that are more logical and objective by nature—finance, manufacturing, legal, and technical to name a few—often emphasize consistent policies and standards, as well as a bottom-line approach to decisions. Businesses that deal with human concerns—health care, education, service industries, and nonprofit organizations—often emphasize considering the different circumstances of those they serve. As usual, neither is better than the other, but intentional leaders understand their own natural tendencies and work to stay open to the wisdom of the other side when situations call for it. Too much logical objectivity, and people are treated like machines when in fact organizations run on relationships and people aren't necessarily logical. Too much emphasis on values and harmony, and organizations start avoiding the tough decisions needed to reach overall business goals. Great leaders keep both lenses in mind as they make decisions.

When people say, "I always consider both sides," I ask them to ponder where their minds go first: sticking to a rule or making an exception? Leaders who assume they are balanced are often more vulnerable to lopsided decisions.

Consider again the leadership priorities connected with this lens that appear in the chart that follows: fair-mindedness and empathy. Which do you honor more in your current role? Were these part of your top ten priorities?

Logic	Values
Fair-mindedness	*Empathy*
I believe in calmness and objectivity, using consistent standards so that my decisions and actions are fair, just, and effective.	My style emphasizes stepping into the shoes of others and understanding their experiences, values, and points of view.

Are you more like Elaine or Evan? Which of these stories resonates with you more? Remember, it's really quite impossible to be both objective and subjective at the same time; realizing your natural tendency lessens the chance of ignoring the wisdom of the other side when situations are stressful. Which way do you lean?

- Do you first think of the if/then and pros/cons (like Elaine), or do you first think of individual needs (like Evan)?

- Do you prioritize business goals and external incentives (like Elaine), or do you prioritize internal motivators (like Evan)?

- Do you honor universal rules (like Elaine), or do you honor individual circumstances (like Evan)?

Considering these different options, where would you place yourself on the following scale—more like Elaine or more like Evan?

Coaching Yourself as an Intentional Leader

Before considering the options for developing your ability to use the logic/values leadership lens, consider the following:

- What are your goals? Do you need to improve your if/then, pros/cons reasoning or your consideration of how individuals might be affected by certain decisions? Do you stop to consider which of your biases (we all have them!) might interfere with objectivity? Do you too often stand firm or too often make exceptions? Are you seeking a better balance between the easy-to-measure material rewards and staying consistent with who you intend to be?

- For most kinds of leaders, empathy matters. For those who aspire to high-level, visionary leadership, the component of EQ that matters most is empathy.[3]

Check your type page in the appendix (page 151) for information about your learning style. How might you alter the options in the upcoming "how to" sections to better meet your style without overlooking great opportunities to stretch?

A Tool for Balanced Decisions

Type theory provides a wonderful tool for improving your ability to make decisions. Researchers have found that if we aren't aware of the benefits that Sensing, Intuition, Thinking, and Feeling each add to the decision-making process, we're likely to spend 90 percent of our effort on the preferences we favor and gloss over the rest. Think of how Elaine and Evan might have benefited from thinking through these questions. (Note that this was the process I used with Kent on page 64):

- Sensing
  - What are the facts in this situation?
  - What problem are we really trying to solve?
- Intuition
  - Is this problem analogous to any we've seen before?
  - What possible ways could we solve it?
- Thinking
  - What objective criteria might we use to evaluate our choices?
  - What are the pros and cons of each option?
- Feeling
  - What values are most important to consider in this decision?
  - Who are the stakeholders and what are their values that we need to consider?

Opportunities for Improving Your Focus on Logic

Master deliberate tools. Get used to thinking, "If I do this, then _____ might happen." "What are the pros and cons of each choice?" Or, build a matrix. List the options in a column. Label the other columns with the most important criteria you'll consider. Then, rank the options based on each criteria. Which, overall, receives the best rating?

Re-evaluate a past decision. Choose a decision you weren't particularly happy with. Were there unintended consequences? What precedents might you have set? Reconsider the decision using the questions listed above. What elements of decision-making might you have glossed over?

Know your facts. Part of building assertiveness is being confident about the information you have. Often, though, people haven't sorted through facts versus opinions. If you need to present your decision to someone else, or take a stand, write out what you think you know and how you know it is true. Then, label each item as a fact or an opinion. Where might you need research to prove or disprove the opinions? Do you need to gather more factual information?

Evaluate extrinsic rewards. Sometimes if leaders or organizations overemphasize altruism, they can fail to attract talent or build the financial support they need. They may also underestimate the altruism of those who want to make a difference yet also see nothing wrong with being rewarded at the same level as other people with equal talent. Consider reading *Mountains Beyond Mountains* by Tracy Kidder, which tells the story of Paul Farmer, a surgeon and anthropologist who has worked systemically to bring better medicine to Haiti while building a financially sound organization, as an example of mixing altruism with sound business principles.

Work on objectivity. If you naturally empathize with people, learn to ask yourself, "What would someone unfamiliar with this situation observe? How might an objective person counter my concerns? Would any actions I might take that come from empathizing actually be harmful in the long run?" (Think back to the community relations team that needed to resolve its conflicts more than its members needed empathy.)

Options for Improving Your Focus on Values

List the stakeholders. Think through a past decision where the outcome might have been better. Who were the stakeholders? Did they have issues or concerns that weren't factored into the decision-making process? How did that affect acceptance or implementation of the decision?

Work on empathy. As it is defined in EQ, "Empathy has relatively little to do with objective truth. Rather, it hinges on grasping the other's subjective truth."[4] For those who value logic, it can, for example, be very difficult to ignore obvious logical consequences and instead unearth the beliefs another person holds about probable consequences. With whom could you meet to practice that skill? Avoid any drive to solve a problem or reinterpret a situation. Simply listen and seek to revoice and understand ideas and concerns.

Identify your intrinsic goals. Review the forty leadership priorities (pages 3–5 and pages 168–169 in the appendix), focusing on the prompt, "When I retire, I want to be able to say I led with_____" or "No matter where or who I lead, I want to value _____." What adjustments do you need to make in your style to ensure that you reach these goals?

Balance the emotional quotient competencies of self-regard, independence, and assertiveness. Frequently, people whose emotional intelligence is well developed in self-regard, independence, and assertiveness have a harder time with empathy.[5] Consider whether this is true for you and then think of specifics. When has your own self-regard or natural assertiveness blocked you from thinking about how other people might be affected by a situation? Did your ability to grasp reality frustrate you when others were ignoring time limits or financial restraints or the consequences of their actions? If this rings true, make improving your ability to empathize a priority.

Review real evidence. Logic dictates that corporate downsizing will improve the bottom line. Empirical research shows this is only true in the short term. Long term, downsized companies do less well on average than those who retain employees through thick and thin.[6] Loss of knowledge and a smudged market reputation, among other factors, interfere with predicted cost savings. How often have you or those with whom you lead underestimated the ways in which human factors might interfere with predicted logical results?

> Remember, the logic/values leadership lens helps you manage the tension between universal principles and individual truths. Have you found the right balance for making decisions in your current role?

CHAPTER 10

Balancing Outcomes With People

Lens 8

Thinking	Feeling
Outcomes	People
Results	Harmony

What motivates those you lead, and how does it differ from what makes you tick? Is it the thrill of accomplishing audacious goals or receiving ever-increasing bonus checks? Is it a sense of belonging, of feeling valued, or the fulfillment of working with a great team that brings out the best in each person? While almost everyone craves a bit of both, the dissonance of working in an environment with contrary definitions of success is a major source of job dissatisfaction.

With the publication of Walter Isaacson's biography of Steve Jobs,[1] both the Emotional Intelligence Connection group and MBTI Professionals group on LinkedIn held lively discussions about Jobs's "success oriented" style and EQ. Was his abrasive leadership style key to his success? Two schools of thought emerge in the numerous postings:

- Yes. In the highly competitive, rapidly changing environment of Apple, Jobs's demands on those who worked for him kept Apple at the forefront. After all, no one really had to put up with his abuse—they were all talented enough to go elsewhere. By staying, though, they learned to demand more of themselves. As Mike Hoban summarized in an article for *Fast Company*, "I'm suggesting that a less edgy, less intense, less arrogant, less dogmatic Steve Jobs would not likely have achieved the results he did. In fact, his towering strengths—the brilliance, the focus on being both aspirational and inspirational, the tenacity—could not have played out the way they did if he had controlled his 'dark side.'" He compared the trust/fear relationship Jobs had with several employees to the thrills/fears of bungee jumping.[2]

- No. What could Apple have accomplished if Jobs had developed more emotional intelligence? Might his teams have avoided major failures? (Remember, the Mac was second to PCs for decades, NeXT was not a success, and Jobs was actually fired.) While we'll never know, it is most likely true that trying to "be like Jobs" in leadership style without also having his unique genius for details, engineering, and anticipating customer usage is a recipe for disaster.

With this lens, leaders can consider *both* sources of motivation: the excitement and rewards of achievement as well as the satisfaction and fulfillment of being a key member of a team that works well together.

Too Much Focus on Outcomes

Jenny called me in because her managers had stopped working as a team. "When I first took over here," she told me, "they all seemed to like each other. We got things done in meetings.

"Now, though, team meetings can be pretty awful. We've expanded—our business has exploded, really—so there are a lot of new people since you last worked with me. Maybe they just need to understand each other better. You'd think everyone would be happy around here, given the huge bonuses, but judging from their grumbling, I wonder if they resent the new responsibilities our growth requires of them. Two of them complain constantly about everyone else. Maybe if I let that pair go, the team's tone would change for the better."

Jenny detailed a few accounts of unmet deadlines and trust issues. I said, "If we're going to rebuild trust, I'd suggest that I meet with each person to hear their concerns and perspectives."

She nodded, and then added, "Before you do, you should know—I completely lost it at last week's meeting. Yelled at them. Once again, half of them hadn't read information I sent, so they weren't ready to collaborate. I don't know what they think of me now."

As I interviewed each of the nine managers, I heard about the stress of expanding from two to nine locations in just a few years. Most of the managers had changed positions at least twice in that period. They'd also traded assistant managers to give each office enough experienced staff, switched inventory systems, remodeled, and more. And they told me in various ways that Jenny had become a tyrant, totally oblivious to the very real problems they faced with all the changes.

I decided to begin the group session with a timeline—a long paper strip on the wall marked off with each year since Jenny had become their leader. Handing each person several square sticky notes, I said, "There have been lots of changes here. Write each change you've been involved with—new offices, new jobs, new products—on a separate note and place them all on the timeline."

Soon the paper strip was buried in colorful notes. Jenny stared at it and then pulled me aside. "I honestly hadn't thought about this. I stayed in the same office and just gained more of the same kinds of responsibilities. It's been a total madhouse for them, hasn't it?"

The Type/Emotional Quotient Connection

Jenny's competencies in self-management and project management encompassed her favorite leadership activities. Since she did well in these areas, which favored her preference for outcomes, she assumed she was a strong leader and blamed her team for their lack of collaboration. The excitement of success and the monetary rewards were sufficient motivation for her, but essentially blocked her from fully grasping how difficult her team's jobs had become and how little effort she had put into leading change.

While self-regard is essential for leaders (after all, why follow anyone who doesn't believe in herself?), without empathy, Jenny's failure to reflect on the people side of growth made it easy to jump to labels of incompetence rather than stepping into people's shoes. I worked with Jenny and her team for several sessions and the collaboration improved. Jenny, however, eventually decided to change firms. "Something was lost forever when I exploded in that meeting," she told me, "but I honestly don't think I'll make the same mistakes in my new job."

Too Much Focus on People

Jeff, the director of a nonprofit organization, prided himself on inclusion, considering all points of view, allowing processes to shape themselves, and above all, listening when others actively opposed him. This worked well in his environment, where the knowledge and skills of volunteers were as crucial as those of employees. When a group of volunteers asked to have a potentially controversial issue added to a board meeting agenda, he readily agreed.

Jeff then asked his training director to suggest possible processes that would keep the meeting on a positive note. "What if we let all of our volunteers know that we will be asking for their input on several strategic issues?" she suggested.

They quickly put together a plan. Attendees would be able to choose to work in one of several small groups, with each group focusing on a different issue. The groups would then give five-minute reports at the board meeting.

"That way, we'll hear about each issue, even the controversial one, and the board can take all the reports into consideration," Jeff concluded.

The meeting was well attended. The small groups were a success. The reports, however, were a failure. The volunteers who had discussed the divisive issue used their five minutes to call for the resignation of board members who held opposing views. A shouting match ensued until, in desperation, Jeff adjourned the meeting.

Later, Jeff told another board member, "It was all my fault. I should have spent more time with those dissenters so that they understood how sincere we were in listening to their concerns."

"I doubt it," the board member replied, and helped Jeff think through other reasons the dissenting faction had acted as they had. For example, an informal power structure existed among the volunteers. A recent news story had covered how similar tactics worked in another organization. An influential donor had fed some key misinformation to the dissenters. And a former board member had recently sent them a rather disrespectful response. By defining the issue only in terms of his relationship with the dissenters, Jeff had failed to unearth important factors that were key to avoiding continued problems with them, problems that stole time from working on the organization's overall goals.

The Type/Emotional Quotient Connection

While accepting blame is key to leadership, Jeff's strengths in interpersonal skills and collaboration—reflecting his preference for Feeling—kept his focus on meeting processes and acting on his own values. Believing he could maintain harmony in the meeting left him vulnerable to the things he couldn't control; he'd ignored external factors and the business goals of the board meeting when planning.

Using the Outcomes/People Leadership Lens

This is one of the most crucial yet difficult tools to master because while organizations disappear unless goals are reached, reaching those goals requires people to collaborate and not waste energy on conflict. Check the leadership priorities connected with this lens in the chart that follows. Highlight the ones that were in your top ten.

Outcomes	People
Results	*Harmony*
Meeting or exceeding our stated goals is at the top of my priority list.	I work to keep conflict at bay so that people can concentrate on the tasks at hand.

Are you more like Jenny or Jeff? Do you focus on outcomes or people?

- Are your first priorities business goals (like Jenny), or do you believe a harmonious team is the only way to reach business goals (like Jeff)?

- Do you ensure goals can be reached (like Jenny), or do you ensure employees feel valued (like Jeff)?

- Do you reward business success tangibly (like Jenny), or do you reward collaboration and harmony (like Jeff)?

Considering these different options, where would you place yourself on the following scale—more like Jenny or more like Jeff?

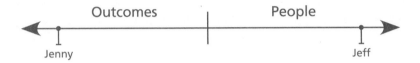

Coaching Yourself as an Intentional Leader

Before considering the options for developing your ability to use the outcomes/people leadership lens, take these steps:

- Consider your goals. Do you need to step into the shoes of those whose motivations are different from your own, whether they're less concerned with measurable success or less concerned with relationships? Do you need to adjust the environment of your workplace to better meet everyone's needs?

- Think through how well you assess your own role in business success and in the harmony of your team. Reflect on a recent situation where things have not gone according to the plan. List what went wrong. Now look at that list and place an *E* in front of external factors that are outside of your control and an *I* in front of the factors that are within your control. If you think your list seems balanced, ponder which items were harder to come up with to understand your natural tendency. Knowing whether you tend to externalize or internalize blame often provides insights for this lens concerning your impact on employee motivation.

Check your type page in the appendix (page 151) for further information about your learning styles and how you might adjust the options for development in the following sections to better meet your needs. Consider, though, whether using one as is might be a good stretch opportunity.

Options for Improving Your Focus on Outcomes

Learn to question. When someone's opinion differs from yours, do you ask questions to see if his or her position holds up to the logic that flows from what you already know? Or, does your desire to maintain harmony keep you from questioning, especially if you fear someone's feelings may be hurt?

If the latter describes you, ponder how questioning can provide insight into the basis for another person's position in ways that increase your ability to empathize and find potential areas for agreement or innovative solutions. Questioning is not negative.

But first, be clear on your own point of view. What influenced it? Experience, knowledge, research, values? Which of these are logical or universal? Where might someone legitimately challenge you?

Second, form questions that will allow you to gather the same kind of information from the other side. You might start a conversation with, "We've both given this issue a lot of thought, and we're both caring and intelligent. It would be helpful to me if we could share how we formed our views, focusing on facts." Explain first how you formed your position, being as brief as possible. Then, as he explains, ask questions and restate his thoughts until he agrees that you understand his point of view.

Think politically. Power struggles are a reality of leadership, no matter how much you believe everyone should be motivated by the common good. Leaders who are too modest about their team's accomplishments may find themselves on the losing side. Speak up about your team's successes. Concentrate on the positive goals of ensuring that you gather needed support and resources for your dreams and block potential attempts to derail them.

Find someone to watch your back. Ask a trusted colleague to pull you aside any time you seem too optimistic or unaware of outside factors that might conflict with your plans. Develop some standard questions to ask your leadership team, or a mentor or coach, to think through potential issues, such as:

- What outside of our team could interfere with our plans and goals?
- Whose interests conflict with ours? What might I watch to avoid being blindsided?
- Whose interests parallel ours? How might we partner or support each other?

Practice championing. Do a reality check on whether your team is truly able to meet its goals, considering the following factors:

- Organizational support
- Time
- Equipment
- Resources
- Current policies

If the team can't meet its goals, who needs to know? What needs to change, the goals or these other factors? Think logically: "If we don't _____, then _____ will happen." "If we _____, this might set a precedent for _____."

Work on assertiveness. First list times that you have stood up for your team's needs and priorities, your values, or decisions. Then, list times that you should have but didn't. Do you see any patterns? For example, do certain individuals intimidate you, or do you tend to ignore small problems regardless of whether they might become big problems? At the core, do you avoid conflict at all costs?

Most people find that assertiveness comes from being clear on goals, understanding the basis of their own position so that they can defend it, and envisioning how they might need to take a stand so they can practice what to say. Apply these factors to a time when you failed to take a stand. What would you do differently? Use this information to ready yourself for a future meeting.

Options for Improving Your Focus on People

Find your fault zone. One key strategy for focusing on the needs of others is ensuring that you accurately identify the role you played in creating a problem situation. When are you most likely to see others' missteps but miss your own? For Jenny, pride in her administrative skills increased her irritation with others' lack of timeliness or preparation while she completely overlooked their needs during change. Again, while we lead through strengths, problems usually arise when we overuse them and thus succumb to a blind spot or weakness. All twelve lenses in this book are designed to help you identify these potential difficulties. If you haven't done so, study the entire list of lenses on page 7 and consider which ones you need the most practice with to improve your ability to empathize and meet the needs of those you lead.

Analyze what isn't going well. Choose a meeting, relationship, or project where you were dissatisfied with the results. List what role you played and what you might have done more effectively. Ignore all external factors and instead concentrate on the impact of your ideas and actions. Where were you to blame?

Practice acknowledgment. Success-oriented leaders often assume that bonuses or other rewards are all people need to stay motivated. However, many people need to hear that their individual and unique contributions are appreciated. Make sure that people know you value their role in team success. Write notes that make specific mention of employees' ideas, efforts, or skills; let senior management know of individual accomplishments; and talk about other contributors out loud in meetings when appropriate. While not everyone is comfortable with public praise, almost everyone wants to hear that their efforts are noticed and make a difference!

Check for fulfillment. It's a fact: doing something for others is more rewarding than serving ourselves. How might your team's goals and efforts—and your own—encompass more social responsibility, another component of emotional intelligence? Whose lives are easier when your work is done well? Who benefits from your products and services? How? In what ways might acknowledging or celebrating this motivate your team?

Study a case. With the goal of providing better support, step into the shoes of an employee who is not doing well. Plan a conversation using these steps:

1. Be specific regarding expectations that aren't being met. Don't say, "You're not working up to speed," but rather, "Your contributions to the last two projects were late, whereas everyone else met the deadlines." Instead of, "Your work quality is poor," quantify with, "I had to spend three hours revising your last report, compared with less than twenty minutes for the others I received."

2. List your assumptions on why this employee is falling short of expectations. Again, try to be specific. Then, brainstorm other possible explanations, including the need for skill development, external factors such as problems at home, and miscommunicated instructions or expectations.

3. Talk with the employee, remaining nonthreatening and calm. Emphasize that you aren't issuing performance warnings but instead working to understand what might be keeping him or her from working up to potential. Solicit specific reasons and possible solutions.

Frequently, when I'm asked to coach underperforming employees, they are lacking a very specific but learnable skill or they have misunderstood their priorities. For example, as I used these conversation steps with a teacher whose performance had been rated unsatisfactory, she realized that she lacked lesson planning skills (yes, she should have mastered this years before, but my only concern was her classroom now). We spent a full day together on class time flow, planning lessons and planning units. From then on, she had control of her class. What appeared to be incompetence was a lack of skill that could be taught and learned.

> Remember, this lens helps you balance business success and workplace harmony. Do you have the right balance in your current situation?

CHAPTER 11

Balancing Individual Trust With Team Trust

Lens 9

Thinking	Feeling
Individual Trust	Team Trust
Expertise, Autonomy	*Appreciation, Collaboration*

My first professional job taught me a lot about trust. I was hired along with four other people. At 8 a.m. every morning, one of the senior managers came by our cubicles to make sure we were working. Obviously, no one trusted us.

Trust, that firm belief in the reliability, authenticity, or talent of someone or something else, doesn't magically appear, but it can disappear almost like magic unless leaders realize that:

- Trust is a two-way street. You need to demonstrate trust to gain trust. We learn to trust when we are trusted and when we learn through experience that others are worthy of our trust.

- Leaders need to attend to three different areas in regards to trust: (1) between themselves and those they lead, (2) among those they lead, and (3) among the leaders of other departments with which their team interacts.

Most, if not all, organizations need all three kinds of trust. Many tasks are better done alone; people are more productive at work when they have more private workspace, a quiet atmosphere, and minimal interruptions, which means we need to trust the people who work for us.[1] Developing expertise in many fields requires coaching, but also lots of solo practice. Leaders need to trust that people working alone are getting things done.

However, we also need each other, and we need others who are different from us. We need people working together. Teams whose members have similar personalities often learn to collaborate quickly, but struggle with good decisions since their natural blind spots are similar. Diverse teams may struggle to build trust and collaboration skills but are often more effective once they learn to collaborate.[2] Further, teams from different departments tend to be different from each other simply because different personalities are attracted to different career tracks. This increases the need for consciously building trust in matrix organizations.

Intentional leaders keep trust in mind from the start of every new relationship, knowing it is easier to build trust than to rebuild it once mistrust permeates the workplace. One of the savviest leaders I ever worked with called me as she started at a new company. She explained, "They hired me because my whole new department is made from the same mould and, well, I don't fit! The team says that they like my offbeat perspectives, but this could easily turn into a disaster without a deep understanding of our differences."

She'd already decided to get everyone off site for two days. "I need a day and a half of purposeful yet engaging teambuilding from you. Then we're doing a treasure hunt. These people are too serious; they can't see how fun on the job builds a true team. I want you to help debrief, tying their new understanding of each other to their treasure hunt interactions and to overall collaboration strategies," she said.

Her plan worked. At the end of the two days, her team understood the way she operated and had a much clearer understanding of how and when team members might partner on projects rather than always work alone, as in the past.

Building individual trust and team trust involves respecting people for their deep expertise, their ability to tap into it, and their self-direction skills. At the same time, people need to trust each other so that when they need to work together, they can. Also, of course, they need to trust their leader. Margaret Wheatley has long emphasized the importance of relationships:

> I look carefully at a workplace's capacity for healthy relationships. Not its organizational form in terms of tasks, functions, span of control, and hierarchies, but things more fundamental to strong relationships. Do people know how to listen and speak to each other? To work well with diverse members?[3]

Are you intentional about trust? All too often, its absence catches leaders off guard.

Too Much Individual

The researchers Nate hired for his new think tank knew how lucky they were to be able to pursue projects of their own design as long as they somehow fell within the company's broad industry reach. No pressure to teach, just research. Everyone was fresh out of graduate school; each had a distinct area of expertise.

Nate also led the department's product development team. He'd managed to procure some of the company's best talent because of his reputation for leaving experts alone to do the work he hired them to do. Further, he had a solid reputation as a mentor. He constantly sought out initiatives and issues that had the attention of senior management, turned them over to his teams, and kept his door open to help when asked.

One day, he called in Kara from the think tank and Jess from the product development team. "A great opportunity came up in a meeting this morning, so I grabbed it for you. The execs want a new model for forecasting profit margins. With your complementary backgrounds, I think that you two could have a prototype for their 2 p.m. meeting tomorrow, as they requested. Thoughts?"

Jess, raising her eyebrows, said, "You're thinking we could build off the model we use for prospectuses? I bet we'd get fairly decent results from the ratio set we rely on most heavily."

"But wouldn't we be putting the ratio analysis to use in a totally different context?" Kara asked. "I would think we'd need to compare that ratio set, and real results, from several past projects. And, unless we try a few other ratio sets, we won't know if the ones you're suggesting are optimal."

"We could," Jess agreed, "but not by tomorrow afternoon. Unless we use what we have, we won't have time to generate a model with even one set of numbers."

Kara stared at Jess for a moment. "I—I don't think I can work with you," she stammered. Jess replied, "You can't work with me, or you don't trust my model? Forget it, that's kind of the same thing."

The Type/Emotional Quotient Connection

Nate placed so much value on autonomy that Kara had no knowledge of Jess's work or appreciation for her expertise in financial modeling. Nate, who leaned toward Thinking over Feeling, just assumed the trust was there. Since all of his team members were highly competent professionals, why wouldn't they trust each other? Here, the stakes were high: Kara didn't want to be teamed with Jess for a rush project bound for the company's president, and Jess did not understand Kara's refusal.

Without any shared experiences to help them learn to trust each other, one could almost predict the initial problems between Kara and Jess by comparing a few of the core values for their type preferences (from the appendix, page 151).

ISTJ (Kara)	INFJ (Jess)
Produces steady, systematic work that yields reliable results	Sees complexities and hidden meanings
Follows a sensible path based on experience	Aligns her work with her ideals
Has skepticism; wants to read the fine print first	Finds harmonious solutions to problems

While type never predicts behavior (the two analysts may have had training in collaboration elsewhere), hopefully this illustrates how leaders can use the framework to heighten their ability to anticipate how people may react. Understanding Kara's reaction is the first step in building trust: she was concerned over the lack of experience they would have with a model they were handing over to senior management—she was not refusing to work with Jess for inconsequential reasons.

Sometimes, though, leaders place too much trust in collaboration.

Too Much Team

Nicole knew her job as chair of the foundation: leading collaboration. Each time the board gathered, she wondered again, "How did we get all of these great minds to say yes to being on the board?" When this group agreed on something, there was little doubt it was in the foundation's best interests.

Meetings were seldom short since Nicole used processes that allowed for everyone to express his or her opinion. Today, though, members were getting feisty over some financial issues. Nicole wasn't sure how to move back to collaborative sharing.

Chris, the foundation's manager, complained to Drake, the financial director, "I know you're head of finance, but I deal with the bank day to day. I don't want you—or any director—contacting our vendors unless I'm in on the conversation. That should seem reasonable."

"Not in finance," Drake shot back. "You left the country before we signed off on several issues. It was my job to ensure that none of the loose ends could get us in trouble."

"You're making me sound incompetent and . . ."

Nicole interrupted, "Let's each weigh in here. It seems reasonable that Chris be our primary vendor contact. Isn't that what we pay him for—to keep operations running smoothly?"

"It doesn't seem like too much to ask," added another director. Others talked about the vendors they had contact with and agreed that working through Chris would in many cases make things easier.

"Drake?" Nicole turned toward him. "What are you thinking?"

"Could we take a quick break?" he responded.

Drake caught Nicole in the hallway and pulled her back into the now-empty conference room. "Have you heard of board fiscal oversight responsibility? I'm here because I know how these things work, and we can't decide oversight matters democratically. We follow best practices, including having more than one person in contact with investment advisors. Please don't tie my hands with a vendor who can inform me on whether everything is being handled above board. I'm not accusing Chris of anything, and have no suspicions, so I didn't want to say all this in front of him. Let me do my job!"

The Type/Emotional Quotient Connection

Like the majority of people who prefer Extraversion and Feeling, Nicole felt that her own wisdom increased when she collaborated. Her emphasis on teamwork left her vulnerable to the dangers of "groupthink" in situations like this. Drake had to pull her aside before she realized he was serious about taking a stand!

In this incident, only Drake had the necessary knowledge to establish appropriate policies. He'd have welcomed questions from the others to try to understand his position, but that's different from taking time to listen to everyone's opinions.

Nicole had bought into the myth that more people always make for more diverse ideas and better decisions; this simply isn't always the case.

- Sometimes individual expertise is more important.
- Sometimes we put forth more effort if results rest solely on our shoulders than if a group is responsible. Subconsciously, in fact, we may avoid doing more than our fair share of the work when we're part of a team.[4]
- No matter how well group norms are constructed, we all prefer to not look stupid. We may hold back our most innovative ideas if we haven't had a chance to ponder and improve them on our own.[5]

Using the Individual Trust/Team Trust Leadership Lens

Different tasks and environments require different levels of autonomy and teamwork, and the requirements can shift drastically over the course of the same project, on the same day, and within the same team. Both Nate and Nicole struggled with this lens because they valued one side so highly that they weren't familiar enough with the other side to use it well. Doing so requires an understanding of when each work style is of most value in your environment, the skills employees need to work autonomously and to collaborate, and whether they have those skills.

What do your top ten leadership priorities say about your use of this lens in your current role? Highlight any priorities in the chart that were in your top ten.

Individual Trust	Team Trust
Expertise	*Appreciation*
I model respect of competency, honoring demonstrated skills, knowledge, work, and results.	I want to create an atmosphere where people demonstrate respect for each other, regardless of expertise.
Autonomy	*Collaboration*
I foster teams where each member can be effective when thinking and acting independently.	I want to foster meaningful teamwork where people enjoy working together and keep everyone's best interests in mind.

Are you more like Nate or Nicole? Which of the following resonate most strongly with you?

- Do you prefer being recognized for your expertise (like Nate) or being appreciated for your contributions (like Nicole)?
- Do you like working alone (like Nate) or working with others (like Nicole)?
- Do you prefer to mentor high achievers (like Nate), or would you rather build a team (like Nicole)?

Consider these questions, and then rate yourself on the following scale: are you more like Nate or Nicole?

Coaching Yourself as an Intentional Leader

Before choosing among the options for developing your ability to use the individual trust/team trust leadership lens, consider the following:

- Where in your current situation do people need to delve deeply with their own expertise, and where do innovation or complex tasks require teamwork? Do your team members have the skills and motivation to work in both modes? Do you have the skills to help them develop skills and motivation?
- Your overall goal should be to build the kind of trust your team needs right now. Do they think you trust them? Do you think they trust you? Do they trust each other?

- Think about the level of depth at which your team members trust each other. Are they able to come to agreement on small issues such as meeting times or sharing resources? On larger issues? Do they willingly share thoughts and ideas and accept suggestions and critiques from each other and from you?

Options for Improving Your Focus on Individual Trust

Examine collaboration efforts. You have learned that individual brainstorming is often more effective than group efforts, that many creative tasks are best done individually, and that most people need solo, deliberate practice to gain expertise. List some of your recent collaborative projects. Might any have benefited from more solo effort? When was team effort helpful? Did it ever get in the way?

Decide independently. Being independent doesn't mean that you ignore the opinions of others. Instead, it means that when you have to act solo, you are comfortable doing so. Pay attention to your reactions. "I'm doing my best, and I have the expertise to choose wisely" usually indicates sufficient independence. But if, when forced to act alone, you become indecisive—afraid of making an incorrect choice—you may need to practice deciding alone. Start small and learn to trust yourself.

Trust your team. If you lead creative, self-motivated individuals, micromanagement is a surefire way to destroy trust. Yet we all know of projects where lone wolves headed off in the wrong direction. Think carefully about the stages at which you want to check alignment between your expectations and team progress. Then, partner on a timeline. The timeline may not always match reality, but it may still provide guidelines for checking in. Clarifying expectations for results and for timing is key to avoiding the kind of over-involvement that leads to resentment and lack of motivation.

Acknowledge expertise. Don't assume people know of their teammates' accomplishments and expertise; some people share successes more frequently, some skills are more visible, and some colleagues have more history with each other. Model how you hope people will share their expertise. And, if you lead a team of experts who tend not to toot their horns, meet with them, and together decide what other team members should know about them. Case in point: I once didn't tell a new colleague that I had significant experience as a consultant. Because he assumed he knew more than I did, at first he thought I was asking for free advice rather than looking for similarities and differences in our approaches.

Avoid micromanaging. People appreciate different levels of oversight and daily accountability. Few take kindly to actions such as the managers at my first professional job who checked whether we were at our desks at 8 a.m. (I was there at 7:42, thanks to bus schedules, but no one noticed that!) Think through how you might be micromanaging. Do you:

- Tell people how things need to be done
- Set timelines for them
- Frequently ask whether they are still on track
- Insist on regularly spaced meetings
- Ask to review drafts, correspondence, and so on

If you say, "But how else will I know what is going on?" consider how things might be if instead you:

- Asked how people plan to do things
- Suggest they provide a realistic time schedule
- Let them know you'll assume they are on track unless they tell you otherwise
- Agree when in the process they should check in with you
- Ask where they might need your input to ensure that your expectations were clear enough for them to complete the assignments in line with any and all requirements

Options for Improving Your Focus on Team Trust

Invest time. When I'm asked to work with a team on collaborative skills, the request is usually, "Can you do a three-hour workshop?" I reply, "What are your goals?" In three hours, I can help people understand themselves a bit better. In six hours, they can gain a basic understanding of team strengths. If they want to actually start improving their collaboration skills, we need at least two days, during which time we can be working on live issues. If trust is an issue, though, two days is just a beginning. Learning to collaborate isn't a quick process. Whether you hire a consultant or work through strategies such as those found in Patrick Lencioni's *Overcoming the Five Dysfunctions of a Team,*[6] be realistic about the time needed to develop trust.

Get help. Teambuilding requires special expertise; we are not born with great communication, conflict resolution, empathy, and listening skills! Further, while leaders can indeed lead their teams through many skill-building endeavors, it is nearly impossible to participate yourself and also observe interactions among individuals and their reactions to your input. Enlisting a facilitator, whether from your human resources department or an outside firm, can be a real benefit to your teambuilding.

Get a framework. Too often, leaders think, "We need something new to hone our skills," so they move from one instrument or theory for group dynamics to the next, never taking time to live with any deeply. I favor Jungian type because after twenty years, I'm still developing and learning about new applications. Check out the Suggestions for Further Reading section of this book (page 149) for a wide variety of applications and to see how you might use the framework again and again, making it part of team culture.

Learn to appreciate. What do you reward and how? People like to be recognized in different ways. And people with different type preferences differ in the kinds of things they wish to be recognized for.

People who prefer Thinking want recognition when they've exceeded expectations. Praise them too much and they'll start wondering what you want from them. Feeling types need to know they are being of service and meeting your needs, so they often want praise along the way. Neither like false or general praise, and both grow resentful if they don't receive appropriate appreciation.

Define the relationships you need for your job. As your roles change, so do the relationships you need. I've often worked with clients who competed with peers only to find themselves managing those peers at a later date. Or, someone who directly reported to a leader is now a peer. Be intentional in considering the new relationship and how to nurture it appropriately.

> Remember, this lens helps you honor individual strengths and initiative while building the atmosphere and trust needed for deep collaboration. Are you striking the right balance in your current environment?

CHAPTER 12

Balancing Planning With Flexibility

Lens 10

Judging	Perceiving
Planning	Flexibility
Organization	*Adaptability*

Do you like to plan ahead or react as things unfold? Here in the United States, planning is almost universally seen as a virtue. Companies forge strategic plans. Parents scold, "Why didn't you plan ahead?" We're told, "Failing to plan is planning to fail."

Still, many religions have some form of the proverb, "Want to make God laugh? Announce your plans." After all, things seldom unfold as predicted. Relying on a plan sometimes keeps us from noting important new information, unanticipated needs, or the necessity of key corrections in course.

Other cultures place a much higher value on responding to the moment. When teaching a workshop for about thirty people in another country, I was asked to begin at 4:30, so I arrived by four to set up. By 4:30, only two people had arrived. Most came around 5:15. At 5:30, after everyone had a chance to settle in with their chosen refreshments, we began. First item on the agenda? My interpreter led a discussion to determine the best starting time for the next three nights. Novel thought, isn't it? Base the schedule on the needs of the particular group attending. Everyone arrived by the agreed-upon time for the subsequent sessions.

If you think that staying flexible is fine for a little set of workshops, but not for anything big, consider how the monumental planning efforts of different nations fed into the disaster of World War I: France only planned for offensive moves, Russia planned for upholding the tradition of their cavalry, England planned for action after establishing certainties, and Germany had books full of plans for just about every contingency.[1] And, none of their plans worked out very well. Is there a happy medium? Maybe Eisenhower put it best: "Plans are worthless, but planning is everything."[2]

Henry Mintzberg, author of *The Rise and Fall of Strategic Planning*, encourages us to think about strategic thinking rather than strategic planning, substituting awareness of what is happening and what just happened, and adjusting accordingly, with emphasis on analyzing and predicting.[3] That's a fair description of how intentional leaders might use this lens.

In my first years of facilitating strategic planning, we devoted the first session with a client to our own version of SWOT analysis—strengths, weaknesses, opportunities, and threats. Then, when driving to the second meeting (most clients were a few hours away), we'd brainstorm the goals we thought our client should set. This was for our eyes, not theirs. Our job was to facilitate the process, not dictate their future, but thinking ahead let us form appropriate guiding questions, consider the organization's unique features, and add enough focus to the process to guarantee success.

Intentional leaders know that you need a plan to recognize when plans aren't working, and thus know when changing horses midstream is indeed not just worth the risk but an imperative.

How much do you plan? Planners come in all shapes and sizes. One of the misconceptions with type theory is that those who prefer Judging are the planners (stereotyped as rigid) and those who prefer Perceiving are in-the-moment (stereotyped as procrastinators). A better way to grasp the difference, though, is to think about:

- Coming to closure (Judging) versus keeping options open (Perceiving)
- Laying out the chunks in a task or project (Judging) or letting projects unfold (Perceiving)
- Working toward a product (Judging) versus working through a process (Perceiving)
- Keeping things under control (Judging) versus readying contingencies just in case (Perceiving)

Planning or being flexible is a fairly good summary of the differences. Let's look at the dilemmas of each with the experiences of Brandon and Brenda.

The Planning Trap

Brandon excelled at strategic planning. He knew better than to plan down to the minute, and instead created flow maps of each planning stage to ensure a creative process. His style was to set agendas with loose time frames that allowed for plenty of unanticipated exploration of new issues or necessary information.

For one in-depth session, as soon as planning team members arrived at the off-site retreat facility, Brandon put them to work, randomly forming groups to analyze existing goals for relevance and the progress made toward them over the prior year. Then in those same groups, they brainstormed answers to the question, "What analogy might guide our conversation? What can help us take a fresh look at our mission, as well as where we hope to be in five years?" When the whole team then came together, fresh energy flowed and the shared analogies brought both laughter and insights. "We are like helicopter parents," one group insisted, citing how they thought their products could do no wrong and deserved special consideration.

With the mission in front of them, team members then took on constituency roles, stepping into the shoes of customers, vendors, employees, and so on. What new goals would meet the needs of these various groups?

Now the walls were filled with ideas. Brandon said, "Obviously we can't do it all. Think about your own area's expertise, resources, commitments, dreams, and goals. Which of the goals is a good fit? Where does your enthusiasm intersect with the organization's needs? Let's start claiming goals and see where the plan goes. Take a good five minutes to read and select. We'll then have time to help each other draft action plans."

No one moved from the room, but only a couple people started selecting goals. Others began side conversations, checked emails, or otherwise disengaged. By the time Brandon called the group back together, the energy level had dropped to zero. When he asked for goal commitments, one person said, "I can't choose yet. I need way more time to set priorities. I know we won't meet face-to-face again for quite some time, but we can finish this up with a conference call." Others nodded.

Brandon felt his heart begin to pound. "We've tried that before, and you know what happens? We get sucked back into our day-to-day emergencies, never finish the action plans, and never move forward. We can't stop yet. Besides, these plans are just outlines of where you *hope* to go, not contracts in blood," he added in desperation. But he could tell by their faces that he was losing the battle.

The Type/Emotional Quotient Connection

Brandon hadn't anticipated the possibility that few would share his desire for closure; he thought that the time he set aside to write action plans would be seen as a gift, not a slapdash rush to the finish. In terms of EQ, Brandon hadn't realized how having his plans go awry increased his stress. Afterward, he admitted that he'd relied too heavily on the meeting format to get people excited about potential goals. He'd had no alternate plan ready to reengage the group.

Take a look at your type page in the appendix (page 151). Note the section, "How Your Type Preferences Work Together," which provides a snapshot of whether you are more open in the internal or external world. Remember, we all have a way to come to judgments and a way to perceive. Brandon's full type code is INFJ. The INFJ page reads:

- In the internal world, you are open, curious, questioning, and flexible.
- To the external world, you appear structured, decisive, and ordered.

Brandon had all kinds of flexible ideas for the meeting while he was planning, but he drove for the goals when in the external world, keeping the meeting moving toward his desired conclusion. Ideally, he needed time to think—to return to his internal world—when things didn't go as planned.

The Flexibility Trap

"This is it!" Brenda, a vice president in her firm's human resources department, told her leadership team when she returned from a conference. "I picked up five or six great employee feedback tools in the sessions I attended. They're designed to guide and motivate skill development instead of the carrot/stick stuff that too many of our department managers still rely on."

The team agreed that the new tools were a vast improvement over their current ad hoc approach. One person suggested, "Perhaps we should develop a new feedback form or process outline—or something—for people to follow as they first try this."

Brenda shook her head. "They can pick and choose among the tools," she said, "so I don't want to create anything that suggests rigidity."

A few weeks later, Brenda and two other members of her leadership team, who had attended full-day workshops on motivational feedback, held a training session on the new tools for all of the managers. Everyone seemed thoroughly engaged in the role-playing and other activities Brenda had designed. But when the next cycle of employee reviews came in, Brenda noticed that they still used the old formats. The managers weren't using the new tools. Brenda shared her frustrations: "No one voiced *any* concerns in the training. Do they need more information?"

The Type/Emotional Quotient Connection

In leaving the managers free to use the tools in any way that met their needs, Brenda neglected to set expectations, let alone suggest an implementation plan. She was right to anticipate that the managers might have different needs, but whereas

Brenda thought she'd conveyed that using the new tools was mandatory, her failure to set expectations conveyed that using the tools was optional.

In contrast to Brandon, Brenda's preferences for Extraversion, Intuition, Feeling, and Perceiving (ENFP) meant that:

- To the external world, Brenda appears open, curious, questioning, and flexible.
- In the internal world, she is structured, decisive, and ordered.

In this instance, she and her team were very certain that the new feedback methods were superior. Brenda needed to leave a bit of her openness behind and instead communicate the problem with the current feedback system, set a clear picture of how the new tools addressed those concerns, lay out options for using them, and perhaps provide a check-in process so individuals could get help figuring out which tools best fit their needs.

Using the Planning/Flexibility Leadership Lens

Perhaps you've heard that knowledge is knowing that the tomato is a fruit; wisdom is not adding tomatoes to a fruit salad. Similarly, planning is the knowledge—the smart thing to do; wisdom is changing plans or even planning to change a plan.

What is your natural stance on planning? Different roles and responsibilities change the scope of necessary planning. Emergency room doctors, for example, may not be able to plan a patient schedule, but they do have plans for prioritizing patients, replenishing supplies, handling natural disasters, and so on.

Check the leadership priorities connected with this lens as you start to ponder how to balance the needs of your current role. Were either of these priorities in your top ten?

Planning	Flexibility
Organization	*Adaptability*
I emphasize thinking through project or systems processes, needs, and expectations to create workable plans and practices.	I model being able to adjust to ever-changing circumstances, responding to the needs of the moment.

Are you more like Brandon or Brenda? Consider these questions:

- Do you "know" how long tasks take (like Brandon), or do you let tasks emerge (like Brenda)?
- Are you stressed by uncertainty (like Brandon), or are you stressed by rigidity (like Brenda)?
- Are you concerned about changing deadlines (like Brandon), or are you concerned about missing opportunities (like Brenda)?

Based on your answers to the questions, where would you place yourself on the following scale? Are you more like Brandon or more like Brenda?

Coaching Yourself as an Intentional Leader

Before you choose among the options in the following section for improving your ability to use the planning/flexibility leadership lens, consider the following:

- Where do your responsibilities benefit from planning? When is openness important? Which is easier for you?
- Are there conflicts on your team concerning this lens? How might you help people see the value of planning and flexibility? Are there trust issues because of different viewpoints on deadlines or closure?

Check the information for your type in the appendix (page 151) to adjust the following strategies to best fit the way you learn. However, also consider stretching yourself by trying something new.

Options for Improving Your Focus on Planning

SayDoCo. In *You Already Know How to Be Great,* Alan Fine provides a framework for working with those who feel constrained by plans and deadlines by asking them to:

- *Say* what they'll do
- *Do* what they say

  Or

- *Co*mmunicate if they find they can't stick to their plan, including a new timeline for the plan[4]

The last step is the key. This framework helps everyone understand that when you ask for plans, you are asking for approximations rather than certainties. Most "planners" say that they know that deadlines are guidelines and that they frequently change them. This is news to their "respond in the moment" colleagues who see setting deadlines as straitjackets.

Plan backward. If planning is one of your least favorite activities, consider planning backward. Think about what needs to be done in a project or a meeting and how long each step might take. If this isn't your strong suit, sit down with someone who does it well to get feedback on your initial draft. Then, work backward from the deadline, fitting in each piece of the project. Make allowance for other things on your plate, including personal commitments. As you finish the process, you should see the actual last moment that you can start and still finish by the given deadline. Often, this is more motivating than simply trying to start as soon as possible.

Think loose/tight. The term *loose/tight leadership* was coined by Abraham Sagie in 1997 to describe granting autonomy in processes while maintaining control of the end goals.[5] Make a practice of minimizing your instructions as to how people will reach goals (be loose) while maximizing clarity around the goals and expectations you have for achieving those goals (be tight).

Be realistic. Consider past projects. How accurate were your estimates of the time and effort involved? Some people seem to almost have a built-in clock that helps them plan out timelines for projects. If this doesn't describe you, run your plans by someone who knows how long things will take.

Think contingencies. Sometimes thinking in advance of potential options to try if things don't go as planned helps people who dislike planning to feel more comfortable with deadlines. One of my colleagues makes contingency plans instead of planning out a project. Where might she get temporary help? Who might do the last steps of research? What could someone else do? Knowing that there are alternatives often motivates her even as she wonders if she's going to finish on time.

Options for Improving Your Focus on Flexibility

Craft for closure. Seldom does any group have all the time it needs to set plans or to carry them out to the best of its members' abilities. Thinking about what closure might look like can help groups keep moving. For example, a technique I've used to help groups move toward strategic planning closure is to write each potential goal on a separate strip of paper, large enough to be read a few feet away. Then, the group sorts them into one of three categories:

1. We are already doing this and need to keep it up.
2. We need to start this immediately.
3. We can't do this right now.

Being able to physically move the strips among the three categories often helps groups finish the process.

Analyze an old plan. How soon do you tend to finalize plans? Take a look at an old plan and consider where leaving options open longer might have resulted in fewer problems, revisions, and lethargy and more innovation, flexibility, and energy. For example, the best trainers I know thoroughly plan the first half of most workshops, but then have several contingencies ready for the second half, depending on the group or team's needs (a major change for one colleague who used to rely on detailed notecards that matched a meticulous plan). Most of them learned to do this after experiences where new priorities or problems surfaced as the team learned more about its unique makeup.

Plan goals, but leave processes open. Often, people who favor flexibility aren't clear enough about expectations. Think through the end results you need. What do people need to know? You can leave processes open yet provide needed guidance by showing samples of exemplary work, clarifying criteria for acceptance, or asking people to restate the goal in their own words to see if their impression concurs with your requirements.

Invite others in sooner. Frequently, people who prefer Introversion like to flesh out plans before seeking input; they need to know what they have in mind before they can ask questions of others. However, they may convey the impression that the plans are set.

Consider asking for advice earlier. Say, "I'm just starting to work on this, and I'm wondering . . ." or "This is just a preliminary idea. How might you proceed? What questions do you have?" Framing your ideas as tentative may make it easier to share them before you've completed a first draft.

Let others choose. Practice flexing by letting others make choices for you in small things. When you're at a restaurant, let someone else order for you. Join a book club where the host chooses the book. Follow someone else's advice when choosing what to wear. Note the unexpected things you enjoy when letting others choose.

> Remember, this lens helps you balance planning and conveying intentions with staying flexible in order to respond to ever-changing environments. Do you have the right balance in your current situation?

CHAPTER 13

Balancing Goal Orientation With Engagement

Lens 11

Judging	Perceiving
Goal Orientation	Engagement
Achievement, Perseverance	*Enjoyment, Fulfillment*

What do you expect from your workplace? This lens is about ensuring that you're on your way to being all that you can be, yet not so blinded by your goals and the effort it will take to reach them that the one-third or more of your time you devote to work becomes drudgery, a life filled with "Thank God it's Friday!"

An intentional leader fosters that same balance for employees after gaining an understanding of their workplace expectations—and those expectations may be shifting rapidly. The last of the Millennial generation (those born between 1980 and 1994) are entering the workforce. Rhetoric in the pop media describes this generation as needing constant praise; expecting fast promotion and having no qualms about changing companies to pursue it; demanding that you meet their needs; and above all, valuing flexibility that allows for work and play.

What, though, do factual data and research say?

There is evidence that Millennials are relatively unjaded. They hope to work within and with organizations to make the world a better place. And they expect corporations to act in ways that are consistent with their espoused missions and values.[1]

They believe that corporations need to be socially responsible. For example, over 90 percent said they would switch the product brands they use based on whether the profits support a good cause.[2]

Millennials seem to be more satisfied with their work environments than previous generations.[3] This may be because they are better at advocating for what they want or, in many cases, what they need to be more productive. Further, given how this generation is successfully advocating for some of the workplace conditions that enable them to be at their best, organizations might, by listening to them, transform their environments into places that are better for everyone.[4]

Wouldn't you like to tailor your work schedule around what makes sense, not a standardized 9 to 5 regimen? Think about how much shorter rush hour would be if every company did this.

Wouldn't you like to work with people who are also friends in an environment that lets you have fun while doing something important?

Don't you love having a say in the projects you'll devote time to?

And since forty hours a week is a third of our waking hours, don't you want to enjoy them?

That's what this lens is about: leading for achievement and *goals* as well as enjoyment and *engagement*. For older generations who only experienced command-and-control, bottom-line–oriented workplaces, a truly engaging environment may seem crazy. Work is work and play is play, right? Perhaps what we're really seeing is a massive pushback against the enshrined archetype of productivity in the workplace.

A Change in Archetypes

Sometimes, looking at cultures, including organizational cultures, through the lens of how and when the various type preferences are honored brings new insights into human interactions.

For decades, experts within the United States community of type practitioners have found that US culture, especially within businesses, has placed more value on Extraversion, Sensing, Thinking, and Judging than on the other preferences. We want Extraverted leaders who speak up and act, we tend to trust empirical data and experience, we emphasize logical reasoning over values-based decisions, and we have an orientation toward managing time and bringing closure.

Perhaps more and more people, especially after Enron and Tyco, 9/11, the dot-com and mortgage industry disasters, and a few decades of experience with the difficulties of two-career families, are recognizing the values of the other preferences, especially:

- Feeling—The Millennials' emphasis on corporate values, human needs, and making a difference reflect the very real contributions to decision-making that Feeling-based criteria add.
- Perceiving—The Millennials' blend of work and play, flexible handling of time, and willingness to let careers unfold as opportunities arise reflect the strengths of an orientation toward openness to what circumstances bring rather than the judging orientation toward closure.

Information gathered from around the world shows that the percentage of leaders in business who prefer both Thinking and Judging varies from 70 to 80 percent, compared with approximately 25 percent of the general population. Sheer numbers mean that the TJ style has been held up as the only way to lead. Perhaps those whose natural preferences provide different perspectives on leadership are now challenging that assumption.

Refer to the appendix and compare some of the values of the ESTJ culture (page 154) with the opposite type INFP (page 155). Here are a few examples.

ESTJs Value . . .	INFPs Value . . .
Objective standards, fairness through rules	Helping people find their potential
Task-focused behavior	Adaptability and openness
Systematic structure; efficiency	An inner compass; being unique
Categorizing aspects of life	Work that lets them express their idealism

Perhaps, then, what we are seeing in this new generation whose members grew up amidst very real chaos, without the stability older generations took for granted, is a call for the workplace to become a place where they can bring their whole selves. Can you lead toward wholeness?

The Upside of Goals *and* the Upside of Engagement

As I considered leaders I've worked with (or read about) who embody the downsides of this lens, only extremes came to mind.

On the "Too Focused on Goals" side, the obvious poster children are the heads of Enron, Tyco, and the financial institutions at the root of the 2008 market crash in the United States.

On the "Too Focused on Engagement" side are a goodly percentage of small startups founded on the enthusiasm of the entrepreneurs who set out to turn excitement into marketable products, yet failed to plan adequately.

Instead of stories, then, let's look at research on the importance of this lens by proposing that it is about sustaining the best of Thinking/Judging leadership while adding the best of Feeling/Perceiving leadership—rather like rolling George Washington and Abraham Lincoln into one president.

From the TJs we need the *goals* attributes of:

- Making decisions based on the verifiable information we have
- Remaining objective, analytical
- Assessing options logically
- Being plan-oriented and organized

In *Great by Choice,* what Collins and Hansen coin the "20 Mile March" captures much of these qualities.[5] Companies need clear performance markers, constraints that keep them focused and within reasonable levels of risk, appropriate time frames, and consistency as they move toward goals. The most successful companies go at a steady pace even if certain conditions urge sprinting ahead.

Yet we also need the FP *engagement* qualities of:

- Exploring options and diverse viewpoints
- Accepting the existence of emotions and their relevance to planning
- Considering the impact of options on people
- Being open and responsive to changing circumstances

In other words, great companies stick to their march, but their march includes the needs of the people involved.

Using this lens well is essential to the EQ realm of reaching goals in ways that make us feel successful and fulfilled. All of us need to believe that the organization we work for has a worthwhile mission and is successfully fulfilling that mission. On the personal level, self-actualization means seeing our potential and believing we are putting it to use. As intentional leaders, fostering self-actualization in employees means helping them see how their efforts are connected with the organizational mission and ensuring that the workplace allows them to find fulfillment in working toward that mission.

Using the Goal Orientation/Engagement Leadership Lens

Take a good look at the values connected with this lens: achievement, perseverance, fulfillment, and enjoyment. Both sides of the lens are crucial.

Have you bought into the myth that you can meet the goals sequentially? First make your millions or achieve some other career goal and then retire to raise a family or found the nonprofit of your dreams? Yes, it worked for Bill Gates, but in

What Should I Do With My Life?, Po Bronson captures how difficult it is for people to make the switch.[6] In fact, it very seldom happens without a crisis. People quit the rat race only after events such as life-threatening illnesses, or coming home to toddlers who screamed in terror at the "stranger," or when asked to do something in such opposition to their values that they could no longer ignore the uneasy feelings their career fostered.

Yet a lack of goals or perseverance leads to chaos as well. Yes, those of us who started our first jobs the day after we graduated from college may gaze with envy at Generation X and Millennials who travel, join in a social cause, or otherwise "defer" their careers or graduate school to take advantage of being unfettered by mortgages, children, or the other trappings of adult life. But eventually, reality needs to settle in.

Were any of the following leadership priorities on your top-ten list? If you chose two on one side and neither on the other, might your personal approach to work or your workplace be out of balance?

Goal Orientation	Engagement
Achievement	*Enjoyment*
I believe in setting worthy goals, planning for how to reach them, and then doing so.	I want to create a work environment that is inspiring, congenial, and playful, where people can find a touch of fun and humor.
Perseverance	*Fulfillment*
I want to model and encourage others in sustaining momentum and having fortitude while making tangible progress.	I want to concentrate my efforts on the dreams and endeavors that bring meaning and purpose to me and to those I lead.

Do you have the traditional goals orientation or the engagement orientation of the new workplace?

- Are you satisfied with keeping work and play separate (like in the traditional workplace), or do you seek to bring your whole self to work (like in the new workplace)?

- Do you have clear goals to achieve (like in the traditional workplace), or do you have clear values to uphold (like in the new workplace)?

- Do you look for individual effort and reward (like in the traditional workplace), or do you value connectedness and synergy (like in the new workplace)?

Which workplace might you naturally create? Considering these different options, where would you place yourself on the following scale—more goal oriented or more engagement oriented?

Coaching Yourself as an Intentional Leader

For this lens, your development options are combined in one group. Achievement and engagement *together* make for a productive, motivated workforce. How can you add the best elements of each?

Options for Successfully Balancing Achievement *and* Engagement

Study ESTJ and INFP. Reflect on the values statements for these two types, found in the appendix on pages 154 to 155. ESTJ is usually cited as the archetypal image of the right way to be in companies in the United States. INFP has no preferences in common with ESTJ. How might each type struggle in your workplace? What is present to help each type thrive? What might you change to allow all type preferences to thrive?

Add to your "top 25" qualities. *Human Resources Executive* surveyed Millennials to identify both what they looked for in companies and which companies they deemed best to work for. Which of the following sampling of the twenty-five factors they identified are present in your workplace? Which might be emphasized more? How might everyone benefit? What concerns would need to be addressed?

- Work schedule flexibility, with the ability to work fewer hours if work is completed faster
- Responsibility and challenges that are given early on in one's career
- Up-to-date technology
- Clear career path options
- Emphasis on workplace relationships, both for teamwork and collegiality
- Challenging, engaging work
- Personal recognition
- Emphasis on corporate social responsibility, perhaps with support for employees who take part in volunteer efforts such as Habitat for Humanity.[7]

Rate your achievement and engagement. Right now, are achievement and engagement in the right balance for you? Check which of the following statements are true for you. Do those you checked in one category outweigh those in the other? If so, do you need to adjust? How?

Achievement and Perseverance

_____ It's easy to plan and achieve career goals to feel successful where I work.

_____ There is a direct relationship between hard work and rewards.

_____ Company policies are fair and evenly enforced.

_____ Keeping work and leisure completely separate works best for me.

_____ I can tangibly see what we accomplish and find it satisfying.

_____ There is support for planning and setting goals.

_____ We are rewarded as individuals.

_____ I can see constant and steady progress as a result of my efforts.

_____ A strong work ethic is encouraged with whatever tasks we are given.

_____ Systems and structures keep things running smoothly and efficiently, so little time is wasted.

Engagement and Personal Development

_____ I look forward to time in my workplace.

_____ I have specific targets for improving my skills and learning new things.

_____ I value my coworkers and enjoy spending time with them.

_____ My company acts on its espoused values.

_____ I can look back and see how I've improved my professionalism over the last five years.

_____ I have access to technology and tools that enhance productivity instead of getting in the way of it.

_____ I'm involved in interesting, challenging projects or tasks.

_____ My company helps us see connections to the overall mission.

_____ My company does its best to treat people as individuals.

_____ It's easy to feel part of something bigger and more valuable to humankind than just my little responsibility.

Take a long view. While our outward orientation toward Judging or Perceiving influences our tendency to form plans or stay open, the timeline we consider is influenced by Sensing and Intuition and has an impact on the processes we use. When planning personal goals, people who prefer Sensing tend to think out six to twelve months, and those who prefer Intuition tend to think out three to five years. Which is true for you? Of course, short-term plans affect long-term possibilities; the two are intertwined.

What do your goals look like? Are you clear about steps to be taken in the near future? Do you also have plans for how to accomplish goals over several years? Where do you need to flesh out plans? How might you better support employees in doing the same?

Ask about engagement. Check with your team members. What small changes might make your workplace more enjoyable? Ask them what objections others might have to their ideas and how they would address these objections.

Their answers might surprise you. Moving the office party from December to January, extending the lunch hour (and adding work time to the start or end of the day) to allow for a workout, starting a sports league team, and hearing more about company support of local charities are a few examples I've heard.

Consider the 20 percent rule. If your company operated like Google, allowing employees to spend up to 20 percent of their time on a company-related project of their own choosing, what would attract your attention? Is there a way you could pursue it?

Allow a flexible schedule. Are you working your ideal schedule? If not, what would it be? What obstacles are in the way? Come up with a set of solutions. Remember that researchers are discovering that Millennials may be happier with their work because they are advocating for their own workplace needs in the name of being more productive and engaged.

Consider what you don't know. Pursuing extra certifications, exploring new tools, networking with people to discover what they mastered on the path to getting the job you'd like to have, and striving for key experiences all take time. Still, they are key to self-actualization and to our capacity to achieve. Identify at least three opportunities with which you might follow through.

Measure with caution. It's easy to measure productivity, income, expenses, and investment in physical assets. It's less easy to measure employee engagement and self-actualization, yet who can dispute the high value to the bottom line of engaged, self-actualized employees who also fully believe in the mission of the organization and are dedicated to seeing it become reality?

What are you measuring? Remember that when we choose what we will measure, it means we aren't measuring something else. For engagement, you might measure the following:

- How many employees seek growth opportunities, such as signing up for seminars, seeking tuition reimbursement, joining mentoring programs, and so on?
- How many employees set their own goals and objectives?

- How many ideas do employees have? Is the company suggestion box used? Do the ideas indicate employees are engaged in the company's overall mission?
- How many employees show up happy and voluntarily at free seminars or lunch events, book clubs, or social gatherings?

> Remember, this lens helps you plan for the long haul, making progress toward where you want to be, while being aware of the present and enjoying the moment. Does your current workplace strike the right balance?

CHAPTER 14
Balancing Limits With Opportunities

Lens 12

Judging	Perceiving
Limits	Opportunities
Balance	*Discovery*

We have limits.

There are twenty-four hours in a day and no more.

We can only earn so many college degrees in our lives.

We can only try so many careers.

Careers place limits on how much time we can spend with family.

Yet the relatively new game of "busy one-upmanship" seems to deny these limits. Frequently, matches occur not only along soccer sidelines, but also in front of office vending machine rows. Players compare volume of emails received, how late they leave the office, how many events for their children or volunteer commitments they'll be dashing to that night, car pool horror stories, or how few times they got to the fitness center that week. Players are docked points for each home-cooked meal they enjoyed with friends or family.

Just kidding, but doesn't it seem as if people aren't just resigned to being crazy busy, but rather in all-out denial about human limitations, especially given how technology enables this behavior? It used to be that only time at the office kept us from our

135

other roles, but now technology tethers us day and night. Jill Andresky, author of *White-Collar Sweatshop,* used one worker's comment on emails and cell phones to title a chapter: "They Used to Use a Ball and Chain."

Here's the big problem with trying to be productive 24/7: It doesn't work.

We act as if productivity can be graphed this way:

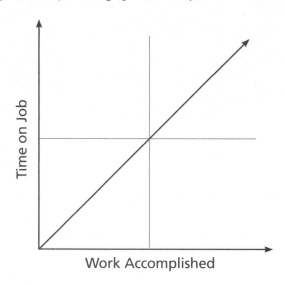

In reality, it looks more like this:

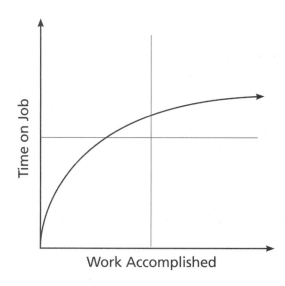

There is only so much we can do. Then our very real physical needs for nutrition, movement, and sleep start interfering with our mental capacities.

Even more important, we need to be more than our jobs. In a 1994 address at the University of Minnesota, Jo-Ida Hansen correctly summarized reality with the title of her speech, "No One Ever Died Wishing They Had Spent More Time in the Office." Still, we're also designed to be curious, to want to settle for more than good enough, and to discover or test out new ideas. We can get stuck in our "balanced" lives and realize all of a sudden that opportunities passed us by.

In *The Way We're Working Isn't Working,*[1] Schwartz, Gomes, and McCarthy challenge leaders to lead the way in creating work environments where workers' needs for health, meaning, purpose, self-expression, and relationships can be met. The goal is a workplace that offers employees a chance for balance, while at the same time opening doors to opportunities. We've already looked at some of these needs:

- Chapters 3, 6, and 13 incorporated some of our spiritual needs for personal growth and for being part of something bigger than ourselves.
- Chapters 4 and 8 addressed some of our need for self-expression.
- Chapters 5, 9, and 11 touched on our emotional needs to connect with and care for others, as well as to be cared for ourselves.

Still, we cannot lead—or follow—without attending to our *physical* needs: nutrition, fitness, and sleep. Not over the long haul. And not without consequences. Nor would the human race survive if we all ignored life outside of work. First, though, let's be realistic about this package of humanness.

Trying to get by on less sleep? Research shows that skipping just one hour of sleep a night results in a 25 percent drop in productivity. In a study of four companies, the average employee reported being an hour short per night. The researchers estimated the cost of lost productivity at between $2,500 and $3,000 per employee, or 54 million dollars a year for these companies.[2]

While leaders can't regulate employee bedtimes, they can emphasize being well-rested, and even encourage our biologically based urge to nap each afternoon. One survey showed that the employees most likely to nap were managers and executives who could hide behind office doors for fifteen to twenty minutes. NASA found that twenty-six-minute naps boosted performance by as much as 34 percent. That means you have a choice: work slowly for ninety minutes, fighting fatigue, or take a catnap, work for sixty minutes and get just about the same amount of work done in that time, while reducing crabbiness and being less accident prone!

Second, what you eat matters. Not only do conditions related to obesity cost US companies 150 billion dollars a year in related health care costs and absenteeism, but also in higher rates of depression. Even if weight isn't a problem, high-sugar or simple carbohydrate snacks, coupled with long intervals in between meals, cause roller-coaster patterns in blood sugar that decrease our ability to pay attention, learn, and follow social cues. Look around your workplace. Is it easy to eat healthy or is grabbing something quick at your desk seen as a virtue?

Third, our bodies were not designed to sit still. We absolutely need at least thirty minutes a day of exercise. Walking will do, and recent studies show that you can even spread that thirty minutes throughout the day, as long as at least ten minutes is at a good, brisk clip. Some companies have gone to walking meetings and discovered that they get things done more quickly when people aren't stuck in chairs. Add in some strength training two or three times a week and you may be amazed at how much more energy you have.

However, even if you hit the gym regularly, evidence says that if you also spend more than twenty-three hours a week at a desk job, you're still 64 percent more likely to die from a heart attack than people who work out and spend less time sitting.[3] Stand, move, wiggle, fidget—people who take frequent breaks even to walk to the coffee maker are far better off physically than those who stay seated.

Chances are, you've worked in an office obsessed with productivity, where demanding long hours and discouraging breaks were the norm. And you may have worked somewhere where what was valued most were multiple methods, new ideas, and a search for options so never-ending that the bottom line tipped from pink toward crimson.

In this last chapter, rather than look at unintentional leaders, we'll look at two leaders who were determined to grasp all the opportunities they could while still keeping life in balance.

The Role of Limits

Mike, a finance team leader, knew his stuff forward and backward. The other managers took working late for granted even as they bemoaned not having enough time for their growing families. Mike, though, insisted that his analysts leave on time.

Of course the team stayed late the night before a big meeting to make sure everything was ready. They came in on the Saturday before the yearly financial plan was due. But Mike likened those events to the kind of overtime that baseball players put in when they make it to the World Series. Extra hours were for extraordinary events.

Mike's line to Dan, his manager, was, "I work second shift at home and it starts at 5:30. Besides, I need daylight to build jungle gyms." Dan, though a new dad himself, usually worked until six or later.

One day, Dan told Mike, "I've talked with the other managers. Each of their teams has put in enough overtime in the past month to earn a few days of vacation. You're catching your regular bus home and you say you're on schedule?"

Mike leaned forward. "Time spent in your chair does not equal work accomplished. Everything gets done."

Late one Friday afternoon, Dan's assistant delivered memos to the analysts: "Please review the attached and change all your reports to match it before Monday. Dan."

Mike learned that Dan wouldn't be in until Tuesday, but he expected a messenger to bring him the new reports at home. One of the other analysts said, "Dan did this just to make us work on a Saturday." Mike shuffled through the pages again and said, "I'll have one of my buddies in the graphics department help us set up a decent template Monday. We'll be a day late, but the reports will be correct. And this is my call. I'll take the blame." True to his word as always, Mike beat the rest of his team to the office Monday and led them through his solid plan for revisions.

Tuesday, Dan hauled the team into a conference room. His eyes narrowed as he said slowly, "I wanted those reports yesterday so I could get my notes ready." His voice grew louder, but Mike interrupted. "Since I ran them with a designer's help yesterday rather than patch them together, they're perfect."

Dan flipped through the top one, then the next, then slowly straightened the pages. He muttered, "I wanted you to work Saturday to finish this. These reports *are* good. But you ignored my wishes and . . ."

Mike said, "You didn't talk to me about it, so I had to use my judgment, not just throw overtime hours at the problem. I have to follow my own priorities, but I want to work *with* you, Dan. On the same team. Why didn't you talk with me Friday?"

After that morning, much of the tension over how little overtime the team put in disappeared as they worked as a true team for the rest of the planning season. Even Dan left closer to five o'clock, more trustful that things were under control.

The Delight of Opportunity

"If all you have is a hammer, everything starts looking like a nail," consultant and author Sandra Hirsh told me during the first of our many collaboration projects. She'd written several books; that project was my first. We had nine months to complete a nine-chapter book. *No problem,* I thought—a chapter a month.

Sandra decided to start with chapter 7, which featured her favorite case study. She wanted to use a theme throughout the book. I suggested solving mysteries because she basically functioned as a detective when resolving organizational issues. "I don't read many mysteries," she commented, "but go ahead and try it."

So I wrote a "mystery" draft of that chapter. Then we tried three or four other themes, all of which consumed about eight weeks of writing time. When we compared them, Sandra agreed, "The mystery theme is probably best, but let's try chapter 4 with it and get feedback from colleagues on whether it works."

By the time we'd gotten feedback, polished chapters 4 and 7 to incorporate the suggestions, met with a group of executive coaches for their input on making the book more helpful, and researched literature to make sure we incorporated the latest findings, about seven months had gone by.

And the other seven chapters? What happened with only two months to go?

They just about wrote themselves. Taking time with chapters 4 and 7 had put us in lock-step agreement on how to present the cases. If we'd done a chapter a month, we'd have spent far more time revising every single chapter rather than the concentrated time we spent on the two that cemented the book's entire contents.

Every time we worked together, Sandra looked to add a new instrument or theory, speak with people from diverse industries, or check with consultants in other countries. She did tell me, "I rely on you to warn me when enough is enough—when it's time to stick to a plan or miss the deadline."

Sandra's delight in discovery meant that she constantly explored new ways to use her expertise, and brought me along for the ride. We explored how type concepts influenced people's approaches to spirituality, to writing, to working with other cultures, to finding meaning and purpose—all of which led to new opportunities for writing and training, to contacts with fascinating new organizations and people, and to what still seems like limitless chances to learn and then pass it on.

The Type/Emotional Quotient Connection

From Mike, we learned that staying in balance takes teamwork, performance excellence, and a plan. From Sandra, we learned that exploring multiple perspectives and resources, trying different approaches, and seeking input can save as much time as planning can while opening up new horizons and opportunities.

Using the Limit/Opportunity Lens

We can't do it all, but how we choose to balance it brings together all of the EQs as we consider whether or not we are pursuing happiness.

As leaders, we're modeling what is possible, which includes intentionally creating an environment where balance and discovery can exist. Instead of aiming for increased productivity, aim for meeting employee needs so they can give their all when at work and still have time to discover all they were meant to be.

Start with yourself. Are you modeling satisfactory negotiation of all of your roles? And even as you maximize productivity to make balance possible, are you also keeping open paths for new discovery that might just add to your success?

Limits	Opportunities
Balance	*Discovery*
I want to model limits on work so that I and those with whom I work make time for family, health, leisure pursuits, nature, and relationships.	I explore choices, options, resources, learning opportunities, networks, friendships, theories, ideas, and so on; searching energizes me.

Are you finding pathways to balance for you and those who work for you? And are you also maintaining the excitement and energy that come with discovery? Are you like Mike and Sandra?

Options for Improving Your Focus on Balance

Consider an individual's needs. Think about someone who reports directly to you who isn't performing up to expectations. Does he or she have a need that might be going unanswered? A physical need for sleep, movement, or nutrition? A need for self-expression? For feeling connected to others? Now, consider whether there are ways you might change the environment so it is easier for this person's needs to be met. Schwartz, Gomes, and McCarthy comment, "'How can we get more out of our people?' leaders regularly ask us. We suggest they pose a different question: 'How can I more intentionally invest in meeting the multidimensional needs of my employees so they're freed, fueled and inspired to bring the best of themselves to work every day?'"[4]

Turn off technology. We're designed to focus intensely for periods of about ninety minutes. Then we need a break. However, we can't focus with email alerts, cell phones, and other interruptions. Set a norm in your office of concentrated effort. Answer emails in batches—your productivity may increase by as much as 20 percent. If you're worried that people may want an instant reply, set an away message that indicates you will answer within a few hours, but to call if they need immediate answers. People who have done this find that almost no one calls; few needs are that urgent.

Allow headsets that help employees use music to block out distractions. Let them leave their desks and work elsewhere if it helps them concentrate. Suggest that they post signs that say, "Working. Interrupt me at _____ o'clock."

Do an energy audit. The Energy Project, www.theenergyproject.com, offers a free online survey that provides feedback on how well you're meeting your own physical, emotional, mental, and spiritual needs. Take the survey and then explore resources for meeting your needs.

Check your time. Ideally, what percentage of your time would you spend at work? In physical activity? With people who are important to you? On whatever other roles or activities are essential to your happiness? Now, take a good look at your weekly calendar. Are there gaps between ideal and real? How might you close those gaps?

Handle stress. Identifying the factors that make stressful situations even more stressful for you is key to being able to handle them. For example, revisit the Change Concerns chart in chapter 2, page 26. Underline any factors that definitely cause you more stress. Then, consider strategies for recognizing them and how you might reduce their effect on you.

Revisit your type page in the appendix (page 151). Often, stress increases when our values are violated. Is this true for any of the values listed for your type? How might you reduce related tensions? Plan ahead. Do you cope best by getting out for a walk, talking things through with a trusted colleague, meditating, heading to a coffee shop to work for an hour, or through some other strategy?

Seek "the zone." Because there are only twenty-four hours in the day, being strategic about how we expand opportunities and go about discovery is key to staying sane. Considering your type preferences can provide clues to what really satisfies you; reread the description for your type in the appendix. The statements reflect values commonly expressed by people who share your preferences. Gordon Lawrence, the author of those values statements, wrote about the practical side of Jung's types:

> The model of development they provide allows us to predict the kinds of circumstances that will enhance or impede development—and that will open and close the door to the zone experience for each type of mental processing. The values and priorities listed in each type description point to the circumstances and conditions that provide that type's motivation. Development and achievement for each type will follow naturally along the path suggested by the description.[5]

If your work life aligns well with the values listed for your type, it's often easy to expand opportunities that are naturally motivating. If work doesn't align well, look for opportunities outside of work that fulfill those values.

Options for Improving Your Focus on Opportunity

Add new perspectives. When was the last time you added to your leadership or professional toolkit? Have you taken courses on new frameworks for leadership, coaching models, or brain research? Have you used your skills in a new environment, perhaps as a volunteer? Check with colleagues, neighbors, or clients—what intriguing options have they discovered recently?

Find some outsiders. Think about joining or forming a group of professionals who aren't tied to a specific industry. Possibilities include university alumni groups, philanthropic organizations, or discussion groups at local museums or libraries. Ask about starting a small group of business people through your church or synagogue or through another avenue. One of my colleagues started a once-a-month breakfast group by asking two friends to each invite two friends from diverse career paths, who each invited two more, until they had a core group of around fifteen people. They discuss books, invite speakers, and share their own interests with each other to maintain fresh perspectives on life and work.

Intentionally delay closure. Do you have a strategy for continuing on the journey of discovery when your desire for balance is asking you to "just be done with it"? One strategy is to pause before a project, presentation, or plan is completely finished. Tuck it into a folder and put it in a drawer for a few days or even for a week. Revisiting it often brings fresh perspectives on what does and doesn't work. Rather than rushing to send an email or submit a proposal or set the schedule for a meeting, wait a day. Reflect on what has happened in the meantime or who else you might contact for new information. What might you gain by waiting?

Try three. Especially in your field of expertise, with tasks you do all the time, it's easy to get into a rut. Make yourself think of three new ways to start a talk, run a meeting, meet with an employee—be creative in what you might choose. See what happens.

> Remember, this lens helps you create an environment where you and others can maximize opportunities and minimize regrets by successfully negotiating among the demands of work and other aspects of life. Does your current environment respect human limitations while encouraging excellence?

Intentional Success

Before you close this book, again choose your top ten leadership priorities from the list on pages 3–5, this time setting aside your current role and considering one of the following prompts:

To be the leader I would most want to follow, I need to model . . .

  Or

How would I lead if everything were under my control?

If the list is different from the one you made in chapter 1, is it because studying the 12 Lenses for Leadership changed your emphases? Or is it tough to be the kind of leader you want to be in your current environment?

In pondering these questions, the focus often shifts from leadership as career success to leadership as a calling. Whereas career focuses on increasing responsibilities or salary or mastery of expertise, a calling brings up consideration of such issues as, "Am I doing what I was meant to do? Am I accomplishing the purposes that need to be addressed? When life is through, will I look back and say, 'Yes, I chose wisely?'"

In his book, *What Should I Do With My Life?,* Po Bronson collected over 900 stories from people who were trying to answer the question asked in the book's title.

He writes, "Asking the question aspires to end the conflict between who you are and what you do. Answering the question is the way to protect yourself from being lathed into someone you're not."[1]

The twelve lenses can often help people to stop trying to be someone they aren't. Because it is so easy to get caught up in the ways those around you define fulfillment, hearing what others with similar type preferences have to say about success sometimes helps in identifying what brings meaning to work.

Take a look at the four descriptions of overall success that follow. Start with the description matching the middle two letters of your type. Read slowly. Highlight phrases that resonate. Cross out what doesn't apply. Then read the others. Your own experiences, values, family situations, and so many other factors will influence your views, so you'll probably find that you relate to portions of those descriptions as well. Take care, though, to be true to yourself; don't choose phrases just because you think you should.

- **ST: Did I do what I was supposed to do?** Sensing/Thinking types are often motivated by a clear sense of duty. In the end, a job well done means that they met expectations in every way. They would not view this approach as compliant, allowing others to define their success, but rather as a search for goals, roles, or tasks where they can mark progress and measure success. The biggest block to finding fulfillment may be their own perfectionism; there is always more to do, better ways to do it, and more to learn, especially if one allows life to get out of balance.

- **SF: Did I help anyone?** Success or failure for the Sensing/Feeling types is often measured through knowing the impact they've had on individuals. As leaders, they find fulfillment in meeting the needs of those around them, seeing others grow, and ensuring that they create a community of support and fulfillment for others as well. The biggest block to finding fulfillment may be a society which in general sees money, not serving others, as success. The well-oiled organizations that this kind of leadership engenders aren't as newsworthy as the movers and shakers.

- **NF: Did I make a difference?** The Intuitive/Feeling leaders want to see significant change as a result of their leadership—changes that make the world a better place for people. While the size of their desired sphere of influence varies greatly from their organization to their community to yes, the whole world, fulfillment comes when they direct their talents and efforts to a scope that matches their leadership capacity. Their biggest blocks may be dreaming too big or underestimating the game-playing or politics necessary to influence others to grasp and support their vision.

- **NT: Did I have an impact?** The Intuitive/Thinking leaders are motivated to become as competent as possible in their efforts to influence others. They want to plan, initiate, or lead people in ways that improve systems and structures, or the very way others think. Their biggest blocks may be developing the soft skills necessary to take their visions as far as they can go.

Now, put it all together. Alone or in conversation with someone you trust, look for contradictions between your vision of success and the things you want out of life. Where do they overlap? Where are there conflicts? Where do you need to make adjustments so that when all is said and done, you'll believe you've made wise choices?

The 12 Lenses for Leadership, together with who you are, can help you become who you want to be. Intentionally.

Suggestions for Further Reading

Brue, Suzanne. *The 8 Colors of Fitness: Discover Your Color-Coded Fitness Personality and Create an Exercise Program You'll Never Quit!* Delray Beach, FL: Oakledge Press, 2011.

Heath, Chip, and Dan Heath. *Switch: How to Change Things When Change Is Hard.* New York: Broadway Books, 2010.

Hirsh, Sandra Krebs, and Jane A. G. Kise. *SoulTypes: Matching Your Personality and Spiritual Path.* Minneapolis, MN: Augsburg Fortress, 2006.

Hirsh, Sandra Krebs, and Jane A. G. Kise. *Work It Out: Using Personality Type to Improve Team Performance.* Rev. ed. Mountain View, CA: Davies-Black, 2006.

Hirsh, Sandra Krebs, and Jean Kummerow. *LIFETypes.* New York: Warner Books, 1989.

Kise, Jane A. G. *Differentiated Coaching: A Framework for Helping Teachers Change.* Thousand Oaks, CA: Corwin Press, 2006.

Kise, Jane A. G., and Beth Russell. *Creating a Coaching Culture for Professional Learning Communities.* Bloomington, IN: Solution Tree Press, 2010.

Lawrence, Gordon D. *Finding the Zone: A Whole New Way to Maximize Mental Potential.* New York: Prometheus Books, 2010.

Nardi, Dario. *Neuroscience of Personality: Brain Savvy Insights for All Types of People.* Los Angeles: Radiance House, 2011.

Pearman, Roger P., Michael M. Lombardo, and Robert W. Eichinger. *You: Being More Effective in Your MBTI Type*. Minneapolis, MN: Lominger, 2005.

Pink, Daniel H. *Drive: The Surprising Truth About What Motivates Us*. New York: Riverhead, 2010.

Schwartz, Tony, Jean Gomes, and Catherine McCarthy. *The Way We're Working Isn't Working: The Four Forgotten Needs That Energize Great Performance*. New York: Free Press, 2010.

Stein, Steven J., and Howard E. Book. *The EQ Edge: Emotional Intelligence and Your Success*. Rev. ed. San Francisco: Jossey-Bass, 2006.

Appendix

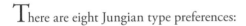

There are eight Jungian type preferences:

- Extraversion (E) and Introversion (I)
- Sensing (S) and Intuition (N)
- Thinking (T) and Feeling (F)
- Judging (J) and Perceiving (P)

The Myers-Briggs Type Indicators used in this appendix are created when one preference is pulled from each of the pairs. Someone whose mental preferences are Extraversion, Intuition, Thinking, and Judging would be identified as ENTJ, our first example.

The type descriptions on the following pages come from Gordon Lawrence's *Descriptions of the 16 Types*[1] (published by the Center for Applications of Psychological Type, Gainesville, Florida) and are reprinted with permission. The neuroscience connections are derived from Dario Nardi's *Neuroscience of Personality: Brain Savvy Insights for All Types of People.*[2]

ENTJ types are intuitive, innovative organizers. Analytical, systematic, and confident, they push to get action on new ideas and challenges. With Extraverted Thinking as their strongest mental process, ENTJs are at their best when they can take charge and set things in logical order. They value:

- Analyzing abstract problems and complex situations
- Foresight; pursuing a vision
- Changing and organizing things to fit their vision
- Putting theory into practice and ideas into action
- Working to a plan and schedule
- Initiating, then delegating
- Efficiency; removing obstacles and confusion
- Probing new possibilities
- Holding self and others to high standards
- Having things settled and closed
- Tough-mindedness, directness, and task-focused behavior
- Objective principles, fairness, and justice
- Assertive, direct action
- Intellectual resourcefulness
- Driving toward broad goals along a logical path
- Designing structures and strategies
- Seeking out logical flaws

Coaching Yourself as an ENTJ

- Choose challenging goals that have immediate application.
- Set aside time to turn learning into strategies and then into action. Usually, ENTJs are motivated to learn cutting-edge techniques that are grounded in sound research.

Neuroscience Connections

Most ENTJs are wired for quick decision-making. They hear or see information, compare it to internalized knowledge and models, and quickly make a decision, engaging only three or four of the sixteen main regions of the brain. This is highly efficient and leads to their strengths in being able to take charge and make things happen. However, for crucial choices, ENTJs might want to consciously set aside time for reflection on logic, the impact on people, future implications, and how different scenarios might play out.

How Your Type Preferences Work Together

Your comfort with using Sensing, Intuition, Thinking, and Feeling most likely follows this pattern:

- Extraverted Thinking leads your personality. To the external world, you appear structured, decisive, and ordered.
- Introverted Intuition is your second function. In the internal world, you are open, curious, questioning, and flexible.
- Sensing and Feeling are more difficult for you to use and may take deliberate practice to use well when needed. While forced overuse can be stressful, *conscious* use is often a source of relaxation.

ISFP types are observant, loyal helpers. They are reflective, realistic, empathic, and patient with details. Shunning disagreements, they are gentle, reserved, and modest. Having Introverted Feeling as their strongest mental process, they are at their best when responding to the needs of others. They value:

- Personal loyalty; a close friend
- Finding delight in the moment
- Seeing what needs doing to improve the moment
- Freedom from organizational constraints
- Working individually
- Peacemaking behind the scenes
- Attentiveness to feelings
- Harmonious, cooperative work settings
- Spontaneous, hands-on exploration
- Gentle, respectful interactions
- Deeply held personal beliefs
- Reserved, reflective behavior
- Practical, useful skills and know-how
- Having their work life be fully consistent with deeply held values
- Showing and receiving appreciation

Coaching Yourself as an ISFP

- Seek out opportunities to learn with people you trust who are learning the same skills. Also, look for strategies that set clear goals and instructions.
- Find settings where you can receive both encouragement and specific yet gracious feedback.

Neuroscience Connections

ISFPs listen with their entire brains to what people are saying, listening for nuances of wording and noting facial expressions and changes in tone, all with the goal of understanding the actions that will be most appropriate. They also choose their words carefully. Note that using the logic centers of the brain requires mastering strategies and concerted effort; logic is often the opposite of acting on the thoughts and feelings of others.

How Your Type Preferences Work Together

Your comfort with using Sensing, Intuition, Thinking, and Feeling most likely follows this pattern:

- Introverted Feeling leads your personality. In the internal world, you appear structured, decisive, and ordered.
- Extraverted Sensing is your second function. To the external world, you are open, curious, questioning, and flexible.
- Intuition and Thinking are more difficult for you to use and may take deliberate practice to use well when needed. While forced overuse can be stressful, *conscious* use is often a source of relaxation.

ESTJ types are fact-minded, practical organizers. Assertive, analytical, and systematic, they push to get things done, working smoothly and efficiently. Having Extraverted Thinking as their strongest mental process, they are at their best when they can take charge and set things in logical order. They value:

- Results; doing and acting
- Planned, organized work and play
- Common-sense practicality
- Consistency and standard procedures
- Concrete, present-day usefulness
- Deciding quickly and logically
- Having things settled and closed
- Rules, objective standards, and fairness according to the rules
- Task-focused behavior
- Directness and tough-mindedness
- Orderliness; no loose ends
- Systematic structure and efficiency
- Categorizing aspects of their life
- Scheduling and monitoring
- Protecting what works

Coaching Yourself as an ESTJ

- Keep practical applications and tangible benefits in mind as you choose developmental activities.
- Set clear goals for yourself. Mapping out a plan, with timelines, for the exercises or strategies you'll use to develop each new practice or skill is usually motivating for ESTJs.

Neuroscience Connections

Observe the speed with which you move to action. Most ESTJs quickly sort through the information they hear and see, process it via the section of the prefrontal cortex that recalls facts and action steps, and move quickly to a decision. You may need to consciously work to consider options other than the first that occurs to you, as well as nonsensory information such as projecting how different options could affect individuals.

How Your Preferences Work Together

Your comfort with using Sensing, Intuition, Thinking, and Feeling most likely follows this pattern:

- Extraverted Thinking leads your personality. To the external world, you appear structured, decisive, and ordered.
- Introverted Sensing is your second function. In the internal world, you are open, curious, questioning, and flexible.
- Intuition and Feeling are more difficult for you to use and may take deliberate practice to use well when needed. While forced overuse can be stressful, *conscious* use is often a source of relaxation.

INFP types are imaginative, independent helpers. Reflective, inquisitive, empathic, and loyal to ideals, they are more tuned to possibilities than practicalities. Having Introverted Feeling as their strongest mental process, they are at their best when they express their inner ideals by helping people. They value:

- Harmony in the inner life of ideas
- Harmonious work settings and working individually
- Seeing the big-picture possibilities
- Creativity, curiosity, and exploring
- Helping people find their potential
- Giving ample time to reflect on decisions
- Adaptability and openness
- Compassion and caring; attention to feelings
- Work that lets them express their idealism
- Gentle, respectful interactions
- An inner compass; being unique
- Showing appreciation and being appreciated
- Ideas, language, and writing
- A close, loyal friend
- Perfecting what is important

Coaching Yourself as an INFP

- Independent study is often your best mode of learning. Limit your goals so that you can explore each one deeply.
- Choose development strategies and activities that allow for creativity as well as flexibility; if you decide to take a workshop or course, identifying how the objectives fit with your values can be motivating.

Neuroscience Connections

INFPs, more than any other type, tend to use several areas of their brain when listening to others; they attend to word meaning, tone of voice, and connections with their values and overall ethics. Values, more than practicality, are important in making decisions. Once INFPs make a decision, they may be less open to new information or the informed opinions of others than people with other mental processes.

How Your Type Preferences Work Together

As an INFP, your comfort with using Sensing, Intuition, Thinking, and Feeling most likely follows this pattern:

- Introverted Feeling leads your personality. In the internal world, you appear structured, decisive, and ordered.
- Extraverted Intuition is your second function. To the external world, you are open, curious, questioning, and flexible.
- Sensing and Thinking are more difficult for you to use and may take deliberate practice to use well when needed. While forced overuse can be stressful, *conscious* use is often a source of relaxation.

ESFJ types are practical harmonizers and workers with people. Sociable, orderly, and opinioned, they are conscientious, realistic, and well tuned to the here and now. Having Extraverted Feeling as their strongest mental process, they are at their best when responsible for winning people's cooperation with personal caring and practical help. They value:

- An active, sociable life, with many relationships
- A concrete, present-day view of life
- Making daily routines into gracious living
- Staying closely tuned to people they care about so as to avoid interpersonal troubles
- Talking out problems cooperatively and caringly
- Approaching problems through rules, authority, and standard procedures
- Caring, compassion, and tactfulness
- Helping organizations serve their members well
- Responsiveness to others and to traditions
- Being prepared and reliability in tangible, daily work
- Loyalty and faithfulness
- Practical skillfulness grounded in experience
- Structured learning in a humane setting
- Appreciation

Coaching Yourself as an ESFJ

- Find and study role models that you admire and whose styles are similar to yours. If you can't talk with those people about how they developed their leadership strengths, discuss their style with others who know them.
- Seek scheduled, structured learning opportunities. Take a workshop or a class, or meet weekly with a peer who has similar goals. Make sure that these opportunities provide for kind, helpful feedback.

Neuroscience Connections

ESFJs can move quickly to action, taking in sensory information, then processing it through the area of the brain that recalls facts and processes, and deciding what needs to be done. The other regions that are most active consider the ethics of those choices, especially concerning whether people are being treated well and fairly. Note that in your desire to explain your choices, you may self-disclose more than other types.

How Your Type Preferences Work Together

Your comfort with using Sensing, Intuition, Thinking, and Feeling most likely follows this pattern:

- Extraverted Feeling leads your personality. To the external world, you appear structured, decisive, and ordered.
- Introverted Sensing is your second function. In the internal world, you are open, curious, questioning, and flexible.
- Intuition and Thinking are more difficult for you to use and may take deliberate practice to use well when needed. While forced overuse can be stressful, *conscious* use is often a source of relaxation.

INTP types are inquisitive analyzers. Reflective, independent, and curious, they are more interested in organizing ideas than situations or people. Having Introverted Thinking as their strongest mental process, they are at their best when following their intellectual curiosity, analyzing complexities to find the underlying logical principles. They value:

- A reserved outer life and an inner life of logical inquiry
- Pursuing interests in depth, with concentration
- Work and play that are intriguing, not routine
- Being free of emotional issues when working
- Working on problems that respond to detached intuitive analysis and theorizing
- Approaching problems by reframing the obvious
- Complex intellectual mysteries
- Being absorbed in abstract, mental work
- Freedom from organizational constraints
- Independence and nonconformance
- Intellectual quickness, ingenuity, invention
- Competence in the world of ideas
- Spontaneous learning by following curiosity and inspirations

Coaching Yourself as an INTP

- Choose a handful of key goals, identify a developmental model that seems intellectually sound, and identify related independent, in-depth activities to pursue.
- INTPs often benefit from skepticism, discussion, and debate. Consider with whom you might discuss your ideas, concerns, progress, or leadership theories.

Neuroscience Connections

INTPs thrive on the logical life of the mind, using the logical reasoning, categorizing, and risk assessment areas of the brain. These areas have little link to sensory input; it is truly an internal journey. Consider how to include important emotions in your analysis and be aware that INTPs tend not to use the listening regions of the brain very actively. Instead, they quickly move to analyzing what has already been said.

How Your Type Preferences Work Together

Your comfort with using Sensing, Intuition, Thinking, and Feeling most likely follows this pattern:

- Introverted Thinking leads your personality. In the internal world, you appear structured, decisive, and ordered.
- Extraverted Intuition is your second function. To the external world, you are open, curious, questioning, and flexible.
- Sensing and Feeling are more difficult for you to use and may take deliberate practice to use well when needed. While forced overuse can be stressful, *conscious* use is often a source of relaxation.

ENFJ types are imaginative harmonizers and workers with people. Expressive, orderly, opinioned, and conscientious, they are curious about new ideas and possibilities. Having Extraverted Feeling as their strongest mental process, they are at their best when responsible for winning people's cooperation with caring insight into their needs. They value:

- Having a wide circle of relationships
- Having a positive, enthusiastic view of life
- Seeing subtleties in people and interactions
- Understanding others' needs and concerns
- An active, energizing social life
- Seeing possibilities in people
- Thorough follow-through on important projects
- Working on several projects at once
- Caring and imaginative problem solving
- Maintaining relationships to make things work
- Shaping organizations to better serve members
- Sociability and responsiveness
- Structured learning in a humane setting
- Caring, compassion, and tactfulness
- Appreciation as the natural means of encouraging improvements

Coaching Yourself as an ENFJ

- Choose development goals that strongly support your personal values or the values you wish to see upheld in your workplace.
- Most ENFJs enjoy collegiality and collaboration. If you can, partner with others while working on new leadership strategies or skills.

Neuroscience Connections

Many ENFJs show a hyper-fast processing pattern in their brains when communicating with and managing people. They hear and see what is going on in the environment, weigh it against their sense of others' motivations and important ethical considerations, and then make a decision. This pattern is key to your ability to meet the needs of others. However, slowing down to consider others' input can be an area for growth.

How Your Type Preferences Work Together

Your comfort with using Sensing, Intuition, Thinking, and Feeling most likely follows this pattern:

- Extraverted Feeling leads your personality. To the external world, you appear structured, decisive, and ordered.
- Introverted Intuition is your second function. In the internal world, you are open, curious, questioning, and flexible.
- Sensing and Thinking are more difficult for you to use and may take deliberate practice to use well when needed. While forced overuse can be stressful, *conscious* use is often a source of relaxation.

ISTP types are practical analyzers. They value exactness and are more interested in organizing data than situations or people. They are reflective, cool, and curious observers of life. Having Introverted Thinking as their strongest mental process, they are at their best when analyzing experience to find the logical order and underlying properties of things. They value:

- A reserved outer life
- Having a concrete, present-day view of life
- Clear, exact facts (a large storehouse of them)
- Looking for efficient, least-effort solutions based on experience
- Knowing how mechanical things work
- Pursuing interests in depth, such as hobbies
- Collecting things of interest
- Working on problems that respond to detached, sequential analysis and adaptability
- Freedom from organizational constraints
- Independence and self-management
- Spontaneous hands-on learning experience
- Having useful technical expertise
- Critical analysis as a means to improving things

Coaching Yourself as an ISTP

- As you choose goals, identify immediate issues or ways to apply your learning.
- Explore a variety of hands-on options for learning: observation, proven exercises, practice, and feedback with someone who has the needed expertise.

Neuroscience Connections

ISTPs thrive on the logical life of the mind, using the logical reasoning, categorizing, and risk-assessment areas of the brain. Usually, ISTPs apply this logic to practical matters such as organizing processes or navigating the environment efficiently. Consider how to include important emotions in your analysis, and be aware that ISTPs tend not to use the listening regions of the brain very actively, instead quickly moving to analyzing what has already been said.

How Your Type Preferences Work Together

Your comfort with using Sensing, Intuition, Thinking, and Feeling most likely follows this pattern:

- Introverted Thinking leads your personality. In the internal world, you appear structured, decisive, and ordered.
- Extraverted Sensing is your second function. To the external world, you are open, curious, questioning, and flexible.
- Intuition and Feeling are more difficult for you to use and may take deliberate practice to use well when needed. While forced overuse can be stressful, *conscious* use is often a source of relaxation.

ESTP types are realistic adapters in the world of material things. Good-natured and easy-going, they are oriented to practical, firsthand experience and highly observant of details of things. Having Extraverted Sensing as their strongest mental process, they are at their best when free to act on impulses, or responding to concrete problems that need solving. They value:

- A life of outward, playful action in the moment
- Being a troubleshooter
- Finding ways to use the existing system
- Clear, concrete, exact facts
- Knowing the way mechanical things work
- Being direct, to the point
- Learning through spontaneous, hands-on action
- Practical action, more than words
- Plunging into new adventures
- Responding to practical needs as they arise
- Seeing the expedient thing and acting on it
- Pursuing immediately useful skills
- Finding fun in their work and sparking others to have fun
- Looking for efficient, least-effort solutions
- Being caught up in enthusiasm

Coaching Yourself as an ESTP

- Choose practical, proven activities to work on strategies and skills. Usually, ESTPs want to experience how things work and will then improvise or develop variations to tailor what they are learning to their own situations.
- Concentrate on goals that apply to your immediate situation and that show tangible results.

Neuroscience Connections

ESTPs are at their best when responding to events in their environment. As they scan for information, every region in their brain shows minimal activity, as if in a "ready" position to activate when they note a situation that requires action. Most ESTPs show more brain activity when looking out a window than when doing rote learning activities sitting down! Look for situations with action and interaction, where your improvisational skills are important.

How Your Type Preferences Work Together

Your comfort with using Sensing, Intuition, Thinking, and Feeling most likely follows this pattern:

- Extraverted Sensing leads your personality. To the external world, you appear open, curious, questioning, and flexible.
- Introverted Thinking is your second function. In the internal world, you are structured, decisive, and ordered.
- Feeling and Intuition are more difficult for you to use and may take deliberate practice to use well when needed. While forced overuse can be stressful, *conscious* use is often a source of relaxation.

INFJ types are people-oriented innovators of ideas. Serious, quietly forceful, and persevering, they are concerned with work that will help in the world and inspire others. Having Introverted Intuition as their strongest mental process, they are at their best when caught up in inspiration, envisioning, and creating ways to empower self and others to lead more meaningful lives. They value:

- A reserved outer life and a spontaneous inner life
- Planning ways to help people improve
- Seeing complexities and hidden meanings
- Understanding others' needs and concerns
- Imaginative ways of saying things
- Planful, independent, academic learning
- Reading, writing, imagining, and academic theories
- Being restrained in outward actions; planful
- Aligning their work with their ideals
- Pursuing and clarifying their ideals
- Taking the long view
- Bringing out the best in others through appreciation
- Finding harmonious solutions to problems
- Being inspired and inspiring others

Coaching Yourself as an INFJ
- In-depth independent study concerning the leadership qualities or skills you wish to develop is often a sure path to success. Make sure, though, to identify clear ways to apply what you are learning in the near future.
- For motivation, concentrate on how meeting your development goals will benefit others.

Neuroscience Connections
INFJs usually need a quiet atmosphere, with minimal interruption, to form their best ideas. They also need a great deal of rich experiences and background information in varied areas. Then, as they focus on a single question or goal, an answer or idea usually pops up. Consider novel problems or situations in leadership to stimulate this kind of thinking. Including empathy and the needs of others in your processes usually improves your creativity.

How Your Type Preferences Work Together
Your comfort with using Sensing, Intuition, Thinking, and Feeling most likely follows this pattern:
- Introverted Intuition leads your personality. In the internal world, you are open, curious, questioning, and flexible.
- Extraverted Feeling is your second function. To the external world, you appear structured, decisive, and ordered.
- Thinking and Sensing are more difficult for you to use and may take deliberate practice to use well when needed. While forced overuse can be stressful, *conscious* use is often a source of relaxation.

ESFP types are realistic adaptors in human relationships. Friendly and easy with people, they are highly observant of their feelings and needs; they are also oriented to practical, firsthand experience. Extraverted Sensing being their strongest mental process, they are at their best when free to act on impulses, responding to needs of the here and now. They value:

- An energetic, sociable life, full of friends and fun
- Performing, entertaining, sharing
- Immediately useful skills; practical know-how
- Learning through spontaneous, hands-on action
- Trust and generosity; openness
- Patterning themselves after those they admire
- Concrete, practical knowledge; resourcefulness
- Caring, kindness, support, appreciation
- Freedom from irrelevant rules
- Handling immediate, practical problems and crises
- Seeing tangible realities and least-effort solutions
- Showing and receiving appreciation
- Making the most of the moment; adaptability
- Being caught up in enthusiasm
- Easing and brightening work and play

Coaching Yourself as an ESFP

- Chances are, you'll find it easier to pursue development goals if you find a partner or a mentor who can add fun as well as provide warm and responsive feedback.
- Make sure you concentrate on concrete tasks with immediate application. Usually, once you engage in a proven process, you excel at adjusting it to fit the needs of a particular situation.

Neuroscience Connections

ESFPs are at their best when responding to the needs of people in their environment. As they scan for information, every region in their brain shows minimal activity, as if in a ready position to activate when they note a situation that requires action. Most ESFPs show more brain activity when looking out a window than when doing rote learning activities sitting down! Look for situations where you can interact with others and your improvisational skills are important.

How Your Type Preferences Work Together

Your comfort with using Sensing, Intuition, Thinking, and Feeling most likely follows this pattern:

- Extraverted Sensing leads your personality. To the external world, you appear open, curious, questioning, and flexible.
- Introverted Feeling is your second function. In the internal world, you are structured, decisive, and ordered.
- Thinking and Intuition are more difficult for you to use and may take deliberate practice to use well when needed. While forced overuse can be stressful, *conscious* use is often a source of relaxation.

INTJ types are logical, critical, and decisive innovators of ideas. Serious, intent, very independent, and concerned with organization, they are determined, often stubborn. With Introverted Intuition as their strongest mental process, they are at their best when inspiration turns insights into ideas and plans for improving human knowledge and systems. They value:

- A restrained, organized outer life; a spontaneous, intuitive inner life
- Conceptual skills, theorizing
- Planful, independent, academic learning
- Skepticism, critical analysis, and objective principles
- Originality; independence of mind
- Intellectual quickness and ingenuity
- Nonemotional tough-mindedness
- Freedom from interference in projects
- Working to a plan and schedule
- Seeing complexities and hidden meanings
- Improving things by finding flaws
- Probing new possibilities; taking the long view
- Pursuing a vision, foresight, and conceptualizing
- Getting insights to reframe problems

Coaching Yourself as an INTJ

- The intellectual journey is usually as important for INTJs as the practical side of development. For motivation, focus on systems or processes that stimulate creative thinking.
- Set ambitious goals that use your competencies even as you develop new areas of expertise. Independent study of theories or principles, concentrating on long-term implications, often provides needed challenge.

Neuroscience Connections

INTJs usually need a quiet atmosphere, with minimal interruption, to form their best ideas. They also need a great deal of rich experiences and background information in varied areas. Then, as they focus on a single question or goal, an answer or idea usually pops up. Consider novel problems or situations in leadership, especially those involving future implications or questions of efficiency, to stimulate this kind of thinking.

How Your Type Preferences Work Together

Your comfort with using Sensing, Intuition, Thinking, and Feeling most likely follows this pattern:

- Introverted Intuition leads your personality. In the internal world, you are open, curious, questioning, and flexible.
- Extraverted Thinking is your second function. To the external world, you appear structured, decisive, and ordered.
- Feeling and Sensing are more difficult for you to use and may take deliberate practice to use well when needed. While forced overuse can be stressful, *conscious* use is often a source of relaxation.

ENTP types are inventive, analytical planners of change. Enthusiastic and independent, they pursue inspiration with impulsive energy and seek to understand and inspire. Extraverted Intuition being their strongest mental process, they are at their best when caught up in the enthusiasm of a new project and promoting its benefits. They value:

- Conceiving of new things and initiating change
- The surge of inspirations and the pull of emerging possibilities
- Analyzing complexities
- Following their insights, wherever they lead
- Finding meaning behind the facts
- Autonomy and openness
- Ingenuity, originality, and a fresh perspective
- Mental models and concepts that explain life
- Fair treatment
- Flexibility and adaptability
- Learning through action, variety, and discovery
- Exploring theories and the meaning behind events
- Improvising and looking for novel ways
- Work made light by inspiration

Coaching Yourself as an ENTP

- Use activities that promote engagement, such as role-playing, ad hoc problem solving, or imagining yourself in different situations. Reflection activities are often very, very difficult for ENTPs, but they are very important.
- Embed rigorous, challenging development activities within a professional goal or project that intrigues you; energy comes from the excitement of creating change. Connecting your efforts to a theory or framework in which you can develop expertise is also helpful.

Neuroscience Connections

ENTPs thrive on diverse input. Their brains are wired for transcontextual thinking: making connections between related, remotely related, and seemingly unrelated things to come up with new ideas. Access information and ideas from a wide variety of disciplines and let the meanings appear. Engage in conversations and brainstorming with people who will challenge your ideas. Allow your imagination to enter into the process.

How the Type Preferences Work Together

Your comfort with using Sensing, Intuition, Thinking, and Feeling most likely follows this pattern:

- Extraverted Intuition leads your personality. To the external world, you appear open, curious, questioning, and flexible.
- Introverted Thinking is your second function. In the internal world, you are structured, decisive, and ordered.
- Feeling and Sensing are more difficult for you to use and may take deliberate practice to use well when needed. While forced overuse can be stressful, *conscious* use is often a source of relaxation.

ISFJ types are sympathetic managers of facts and details who are concerned with people's welfare. They are stable, conservative, dependable, painstaking, and systematic. Having introverted Sensing as their strongest mental process, they are at their best when using their sensible intelligence and practical skills to help others in tangible ways. They value:

- Persevering; enjoying the things of proven value
- Steady, sequential work yielding reliable results
- A controlled, orderly outer life
- Patient, persistent attention to basic needs
- Following a sensible path, based on experience
- A rich memory for concrete facts
- Loyalty and strong relationships
- Consistency and familiarity—the tried and true
- Firsthand experience of what is important
- Compassion, kindness, and caring
- Working to a plan and schedule
- Learning through planned, sequential teaching
- Set routines; common-sense options
- Rules, authority, and set procedures
- Hard work, perseverance

Coaching Yourself as an ISFJ

- Look for organized learning opportunities—workshops, step-by-step methods for learning a new leadership skill, or the incremental plans for change described in *Switch: How to Change Things When Change Is Hard* (Heath and Heath).
- Observe others who exhibit a skill or leadership technique you hope to master. Ask if you can discuss how they implement or plan a specific practice, or request to work with them on a project or activity where you can see them use it.

Neuroscience Connections

ISFJs enjoy learning through activities that provide lots of opportunities for practice. Practice and review seem to help burn neural pathways, which reflect the skills and knowledge in which you have expertise far more than other types. Receiving helpful feedback is also very important. Most ISFJs are very sensitive to feedback and adjust their behavior as they receive it.

How Your Type Preferences Work Together

Your comfort with using Sensing, Intuition, Thinking, and Feeling most likely follows this pattern:

- Introverted Sensing leads your personality. In the internal world, you are open, curious, questioning, and flexible.
- Extraverted Feeling is your second function. To the external world, you appear structured, decisive, and ordered.
- Thinking and Intuition are more difficult for you to use and may take deliberate practice to use well when needed. While forced overuse can be stressful, *conscious* use is often a source of relaxation.

ENFP types are warmly enthusiastic planners of change. Imaginative and individualistic, they pursue inspiration with impulsive energy and seek to understand and inspire others. With Extraverted Intuition as the strongest mental process, they are at their best when caught in the enthusiasm of a project, sparking others to see its benefits. They value:

- The surge of inspirations; the pull of emerging possibilities
- A life of variety, people, and warm relationships
- Following their insights wherever they lead
- Finding meanings behind the facts
- Creativity, originality, and a fresh perspective
- An optimistic, positive, and enthusiastic view of life
- Flexibility and openness
- Exploring, devising, and trying out new things
- Open-ended opportunities and options
- Freedom from the requirements of being practical
- Learning through action, variety, and discovery
- A belief that any obstacles can be overcome
- A focus on people's potentials
- Brainstorming to solve problems
- Work made light and playful by inspiration

Coaching Yourself as an ENFP

- Make sure you involve others, either by practicing new skills with them or by discussing what you are learning. Metaphors, analogies, humor, word play, and role-playing are often helpful as well as fun for you.
- Connect the changes you are trying to make with how they will help you and others in the future. How will they help you widen your impact?

Neuroscience Connections

ENFPs love to explore ideas from their many interests, especially through discussions. Their brains are wired for transcontextual thinking: making connections between related, remotely related, and seemingly unrelated things to come up with new ideas. Access information and ideas from a wide variety of disciplines and let the meanings appear. Brainstorm with others who are as enthusiastic as you are. Allow your imagination to enter into the process.

How Your Type Preferences Work Together

Your comfort with using Sensing, Intuition, Thinking, and Feeling most likely follows this pattern:

- Extraverted Intuition leads your personality. To the external world, you appear open, curious, questioning, and flexible.
- Introverted Feeling is your second function. In the internal world, you are structured, decisive, and ordered.
- Thinking and Sensing are more difficult for you to use and may take deliberate practice to use well when needed. While forced overuse can be stressful, *conscious* use is often a source of relaxation.

ISTJ types are analytical managers of facts and details. They are dependable, conservative, systematic, painstaking, decisive, and stable. Having Introverted Sensing as their strongest mental process, they are at their best when charged with organizing and maintaining data and material important to others and to themselves. They value:

- Steady, systematic work that yields reliable results
- A controlled outer life grounded in the present
- Following a sensible path based on experience
- Concrete, exact, immediately useful facts and skills
- Consistency and familiarity—the tried and true
- A concrete, present-day view of life
- Working to a plan and schedule
- Preserving and enjoying things of proven value
- Proven systems, common-sense options
- Freedom from emotionality when making decisions
- Learning through planned, sequential teaching
- Skepticism; wanting to read the fine print first
- A focus on hard work, perseverance
- Quiet, logical, and detached problem solving
- Serious and focused work and play

Coaching Yourself as an ISTJ

- ISTJs often enjoy working with someone they consider an expert in the skills or strategies they are practicing. Seek out a mentor or participate in a workshop that has a proven track record.
- Consider making a plan for yourself that begins with foundational ways to use a skill and moves to increasingly complex applications, with goals and timelines.

Neuroscience Connections

For ISTJs, practice and review seem to help burn neural pathways, which reflect the skills and knowledge where you have expertise far more than other types. Look for effective processes and key information that you can memorize, since factual recall is usually a strength. Receiving helpful feedback is also very important. Most ISTJs are very sensitive to feedback and adjust their behavior as they receive it.

How Your Type Preferences Work Together

Your comfort with using Sensing, Intuition, Thinking, and Feeling most likely follows this pattern:

- Introverted Sensing leads your personality. In the internal world, you are open, curious, questioning, and flexible.
- Extraverted Thinking is your second function. To the external world, you appear structured, decisive, and ordered.
- Feeling and Intuition are more difficult for you to use and may take deliberate practice to use well when needed. While forced overuse can be stressful, *conscious* use is often a source of relaxation.

1. **Accountability**: I establish realistic expectations and responsibility for outcomes, striving for clarity regarding what is and isn't under our control.

2. **Achievement**: I believe in setting worthy goals, planning for how to reach them, and then doing so.

3. **Adaptability**: I model being able to adjust to ever-changing circumstances, responding to the needs of the moment.

4. **Appreciation**: I want to create an atmosphere where people demonstrate respect for each other, regardless of expertise.

5. **Autonomy**: I foster teams in which each member can be effective when thinking and acting independently.

6. **Balance**: I want to model limits on work so that I and those with whom I work make time for family, health, leisure pursuits, nature, and relationships.

7. **Challenge**: I'm motivated by exciting problems or difficult, risk-filled tasks that enhance skills and prove competency.

8. **Collaboration**: I want to foster meaningful teamwork where people enjoy working together and keep everyone's best interests in mind.

9. **Connecting**: I believe that listening to understand the viewpoints, feelings, and aspirations of those I lead increases my effectiveness.

10. **Creativity with the known**: I value using sound judgment, proven routines, and known information for continuous improvement in practical matters.

11. **Creativity with the new**: I value using my imagination and inspirations to devise original ideas, theories, tools, methods, or plans that bring about change.

12. **Depth**: I want to be in charge of long-term, significant projects for which we pursue a major goal or develop important expertise.

13. **Dependability**: I want to be known as trustworthy and reliable, carrying out the charges I have been given.

14. **Discovery**: I explore choices, options, resources, learning opportunities, networks, friendships, theories, ideas, and so on; searching energizes me.

15. **Efficiency**: I want to organize our work environments, processes, tasks, and such, so that goals are met with little waste of time, talent, or materials.

16. **Empathy**: My style emphasizes stepping into the shoes of others and understanding their experiences, values, and points of view.

17. **Empowering**: I strive to enable others to learn to lead themselves and take the initiative in their work.

18. **Enjoyment**: I want to create a work environment that is inspiring, congenial, and playful, where people can find a touch of fun and humor.

19. **Experience**: I thrive when using our knowledge and past work, which are key to improving performance or to planning and implementing new but related work.

40 LEADERSHIP PRIORITIES

20. **Expertise**: I model respect of competency, honoring demonstrated skills, knowledge, work, and results.

21. **Fair-mindedness**: I believe in calmness and objectivity, using consistent standards so that my decisions and actions are fair, just, and effective.

22. **Fulfillment**: I want to concentrate my efforts on the dreams and endeavors that bring meaning and purpose to me and to those I lead.

23. **Harmony**: I work to keep conflict at bay so that people can concentrate on the tasks at hand.

24. **Individuality**: I value opportunities for solo efforts, making the most of each person's unique gifts, creativity, and inspirations.

25. **Influence**: I want to see my ideas, tools, or plans being used by others to create improvements, efficiencies, or significant change.

26. **Legacy**: I want to be involved in new ideas, paradigm shifts, or solutions to problems that others thought were difficult or even unsolvable.

27. **Loyalty**: I thrive when my skills, experience, and motivations are a long-term match to individuals, organizations, or causes.

28. **Mentoring**: One of my major responsibilities as a leader is guiding or supporting others in identifying their goals and developing their potential.

29. **Networking**: I am committed to making connections, sharing resources, and establishing relationships to enhance my team's effectiveness.

30. **Openness**: I seek and ponder contrary data, new perspectives, and other points of view before reaching conclusions.

31. **Optimism**: I want to inspire confidence in those I lead that our efforts will bring success.

32. **Organization**: I emphasize thinking through project or systems processes, needs, and expectations to create workable plans and practices.

33. **Originality**: I value tapping our imaginations, connecting ideas in unusual ways, and using artistic skills or other tools to find unique pathways.

34. **Personal development**: I am committed to continuous improvement of the skills and knowledge I and others need to reach our full potential.

35. **Perseverance**: I want to model and encourage others in sustaining momentum and having fortitude while making tangible progress.

36. **Promoting**: I work to advocate for needed resources and toot our horn externally.

37. **Relationships**: I invest time in building bonds with others for mutual support that can go beyond what might be required for the task at hand.

38. **Results**: Meeting or exceeding our stated goals is at the top of my priority list.

39. **Variety**: I thrive when my role involves a constant flow of new or novel activities, or many different kinds of activities.

40. **Visioning**: I believe in co-creating images of the future that motivate people and then leading them to work toward those common purposes.

Back in Chapter 1, I mentioned that each of the 12 Lenses of Leadership "consists of two opposing tendencies that intentional leaders balance" (p. 6). Another way of saying this is that the lenses are *polarities*—systems of interdependent sets of values and priorities that, over time, need each other.

Here's a quick illustration of a polarity: Take a deep breath. Inhale slowly. Now exhale.

Which is better, inhaling or exhaling?

It's a silly question, isn't it? Our bodies require both. The energy system that is reality for the breathing cycle is best illustrated with an infinity loop, as shown in Figure C1.

Figure C1 A Simple Polarity

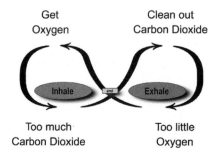

Source: Image template copyright by Polarity Partnerships, LLC

Inhaling brings needed oxygen, but breathing in for too long causes a problem: too much carbon dioxide. Exhaling releases that carbon dioxide, but eventually a new problem will arise: too little oxygen. We can't choose either inhaling or exhaling. Each accurately describes something we need, yet neither is complete without the other. They're interdependent. In fact, you can't exhale unless you've inhaled, nor inhale unless you've exhaled. Polarities are thus part of our lives literally from our first breath. However, learning to handling them *well* can take years.

Barry Johnson coined the term "polarity" as he developed organizational tools for working with these systems.

> Polarities are interdependent pairs that can support each other in pursuit of a common purpose. They can also undermine each other if seen as an either/or problem to solve. Polarities at their essence are unavoidable, unsolvable, unstoppable and indestructible. Most importantly, they can be leveraged for a greater good.[3]

As we've seen, for the 12 Lenses of Leadership, each lens pole holds only a partial solution for leaders. In fact, *if you want to guarantee that you'll fail to reach a leadership goal, build it solidly on the positive results one pole has to offer to the exclusion of the other.*

We all know that either/or thinking can lead to problems—we need *AND* thinking as well. Consider the tensions that arise when we need to honor traditions AND implement needed changes, or work independently AND collaborate, or think short-term AND long-term. In each case, both sides are right. A more appropriate phrasing might be that both sides are accurate, but each is also incomplete. Using the concepts and tools of polarity thinking can help leaders:

- Discern when we are dealing with ongoing polarities rather than problems that can be solved once and for all
- Learn the art of *leveraging* polarities by responding to shifting tensions so that we benefit from what each pole has to offer

POLARITY THINKING AND INTENTIONAL LEADERSHIP

Working With, or Leveraging, Polarities

Our first example, breathing in and out, is a *virtuous cycle* between two polarities; note that the majority of the area inside the infinity loop in Figure C1 encompasses the space above the poles; this represents maximizing the positive sides of inhaling and exhaling. All too often, though, the two sides of a polarity fall into a *vicious cycle,* occupying the negative space below the poles.

Think for a moment about the tension between *Activity AND Rest* for someone whose goal is to finish a marathon. In Figure C2, the person has achieved balance—a virtuous cycle of intense training AND rest that allows muscles to both recover and increase in strength.

But the person shown in Figure C3 is training too hard. Too much training leads to achy muscles and exhaustion, and even perhaps injury, forcing rest. Too much rest stymies optimal training, and the person spirals down, caught in a vicious cycle, unable to complete the marathon. The infinity loop balloons into the lower half of the map. Every athlete leverages this polarity, but not all leverage it well enough to optimize performance.

Likewise, leaders work within many polarities. However, just as working within the *Activity AND Rest* polarity doesn't automatically lead to winning a marathon, simply working with leadership polarities doesn't automatically lead to intentional leadership. Let's look at the steps that take us toward virtuous, not vicious cycles.

The Core Tools for Polarity Thinking

Remember the research cited back in Chapter 7 that downsized companies do less well on average than those that retain employees through thick and thin (p. 97)? To illustrate the impact of the Logic *and* Values lens/polarity, we'll simplify the issues involved.

In many downsizings, logic assumes that decreasing personnel costs will improve the bottom line; employee expense is labeled a problem and layoffs are proposed as the solution, shown in Figure C4.

Figure C2 Marathon Virtuous Cycle

Source: Image template copyright by Polarity Partnerships, LLC

Figure C3 Marathon Vicious Cycle

Source: Image template copyright by Polarity Partnerships, LLC

Figure C4 The Problem-Solution Approach

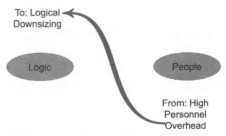

Source: Image template copyright by Polarity Partnerships, LLC

However, layoffs often have a downside: lower morale of those left behind, as shown in Figure C5. All too often, if these kinds of concerns are raised as questions before decisions are made, the askers are viewed as resistant, uninformed, or worse.

If the decrease in morale results in decreased productivity, chances are that this will be seen as a new problem to solve. Perhaps someone will say, "Let's change the incentive program so our employees clearly see how we value them," resulting in movement toward focusing more on people and Values, as shown in Figure C6.

Figure C5 The Downside of Downsizing

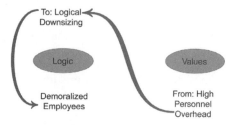

Source: Image template copyright by Polarity Partnerships, LLC

Overdone, payroll costs will again be seen as a problem. Follow the arrows in the Figure C7 and you'll see the "vicious cycle", the infinity loop that will continue without a polarity thinking process to *transform* this into a virtuous cycle.

Intentional Leadership and The Polarity Approach to Continuity and Transformation (PACT™)

In developing his Polarity Approach to Continuity and Transformation (PACT), Barry Johnson embedded the idea that every change process involves some continuity. Intentional Leadership echoes this philosophy with the message that even as we work to avoid blind spot derailments, we lead from strengths. Working with the Intentional Leadership process helps you consider all five steps in the full polarity thinking process that Johnson and his team at Polarity Partnerships call the SMALL process:

- Seeing polarities
- "Mapping"
- Assessing current leveraging of the polarity
- Learning from how we got to where we are
- Leveraging the upsides of both poles

Seeing. The Leadership Lenses and personality type are designed to help you avoid

Figure C6 The New "Solution"

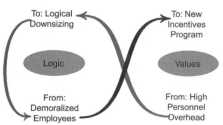

Source: Image template copyright by Polarity Partnerships, LLC

Figure C7 The Vicious Cycle

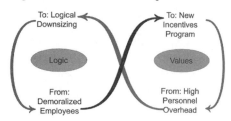

Source: Image template copyright by Polarity Partnerships, LLC

either/or thinking and "See" polarities as the first step. Again, each of the 12 Lenses of Leadership is actually a polarity. So are the personality type preferences described in Chapter 2; in fact, the Logic *and* Values polarity also involves the personality preferences for Thinking *and* Feeling.

Four questions help us see whether the problem we're trying to solve is really a polarity:

- Is it ongoing? Like breathing?
- Are the alternatives interdependent? Like inhaling and exhaling?

Figure C8 Elements of a Polarity Map

Polarity Map™ for Logic and Values

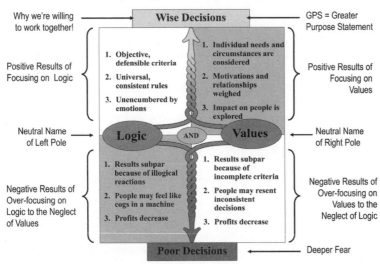

Source: Map template copyright by Polarity Partnerships, LLC

- Over time, are both poles, or solutions, needed?
- Finally, if we focus on only one upside, could we undermine our real goal, referred to in polarity thinking as the Greater Purpose Statement (GPS)?

Mapping. Mapping involves identifying the values and fears of stakeholders as a starting place for constructive dialogue. We need to step into the shoes of people who favor each pole and understand the differences in these two views of the truth that, over time, inform each other. The chapters of *Intentional Leadership* demonstrate the upside and downside of each pole and provide action steps to help you reach goals that involve specific lenses. Thus the contents form a generic "map" of the polarity involved.

Figure C8 provides possible values and fears for the Logic *and* Values polarity and labels each part of the map. Note that every map has the word "AND" in the middle as a constant reminder that to be effective over time, we need both poles. Also note the *Deeper Fear*, an awareness of what might happen if this polarity isn't leveraged.

Assessing. When you sorted your 40 Leadership priorities with a specific leadership goal in mind, and used the chart on page 29 to understand how your top 10 priorities fit with the Leadership Lenses and your own personality type, that gave you good information on whether you were focused on the right priorities. You might also ask trusted colleagues whether you tend to overlook some of the poles.

Other ways of assessing team or organizational effectiveness with leveraging polarities include formal surveys based on the values and fears of each pole* as well as informal dialogue regarding evidence of which values are being honored.

---

*For more information on the formal PACT process, including surveys for common polarities such as continuity and change, centralization and decentralization, or Thinking and Feeling, contact the author at jane@janekise.com or go to www.polaritypartnerships.com

"Learn" *from your priority sort.* In this step, we evaluate the information we have on how well we're handling a polarity. What conclusions might we draw about current and past actions, what caused them, and how can we use this information to move forward?

For Intentional Leadership, part of this step is identifying which lenses are most important right now. There are 12 lenses, two poles each, for a total of 24 potential leadership focuses. Many executive coaches agree that three separate goals are the maximum if a leader is to make progress toward overall desired results. To choose your three lenses wisely, consider whether your biases may have kept you from considering priorities that are key to your goal by asking yourself the following questions:

1. If I focus on the lenses indicated by my priorities, am I overlooking any lens that is vital to success?

2. How do these relate to my personality type? Will accomplishing this goal be natural for me? A stretch?

3. Do I need to focus on my strengths or in this situation could overusing my strengths lead to vulnerability in a key blind spot?

4. Does developing a specific skill need to become a priority focus?

As I coach leaders, they are often torn between choosing lenses that represent strengths and those that encompass blind spots. Which combination works best depends, of course, on the leader, the situation, and the goals.

Figure C9 A Leveraged Plan for Logic and Values

Polarity Map™ for Logic and Values

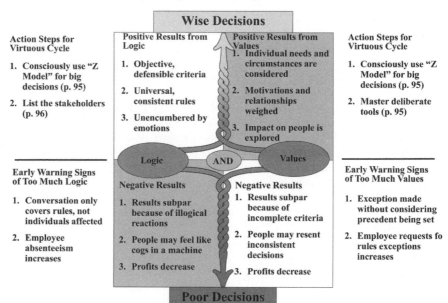

Source: Map template copyright by Polarity Partnerships, LLC

To decide, ask yourself, "If I don't focus on this Leadership Lens in this situation, will I greatly increase my risk of somehow derailing?" Sometimes leaders decide not to focus on a lens that is so much a part of their leadership style that they're sure they will follow through on it no matter what. Sometimes all three lenses match personality preferences. Sometimes all three are counter to preferences. Sometimes choosing *both* poles of a lens is key—and acknowledges the messy fact that leadership priorities can pull us in two directions at once!

Leveraging. Now the real work begins with the last step of the process: leveraging the polarity to transform that vicious cycle into a virtuous cycle. In other words, we want to maximize the upside of each pole while minimizing the downsides. We identify *Action Steps*—concrete actions to maximize positive results from each pole. Some steps capture the energy of both sides—one of these high-leverage action steps is given first in Figure C9. Both the Logic and the Values poles benefit from using the "Z Model" for decision-making described on page 95.

We also need to be able to judge when we're over-focusing on one pole to the neglect of the other—*Early Warning Signs* help us recognize when too much focus is being given to one pole before things get out of hand. Figure C9 provides a complete map, including Action Steps and Early Warning Signs that could fit right into a plan for becoming a more intentional leader.

Capturing the Learning and Leveraging in a Priority Checklist™

Whether you are working with the Leadership Lenses or other polarities, the "leveraging step" concludes with designing an action plan. The suggestions for each lens at the end of the chapters are a great way to begin.

Most of our coaching clients, though, choose to formalize their Intentional Leadership goals with what we call the Priority Checklist™. Different from SMART goals or an action plan, the checklist is designed to remind you day in and day out of your priorities, as well as to let you quickly assess whether you are on track to reach your goal. A sample Checklist is shown in Figure C10, from my own goals for introducing polarity thinking in debates over education reform.

To make your own checklist, use the following process.

First, in 5-7 words, capture the goal you had in mind when you sorted the leadership priority cards. Forcing yourself to carefully choose only a few words is a good exercise in articulating the goal and why it is important.

Then for each lens:

• Choose a priority that will be your main focus. In the example in Figure C10, both Networking and Relationships are priorities that tie to the Outer Focus lens, but in this case Relationships best expresses the focus I need to have. Note that at this point some clients substitute words that are more meaningful to them.

• In 10-15 words, create a statement or question that captures why that priority is so important to your goal. For my Relationships priority, I need to reach out to other influencers, so I wrote, "Who might guide, inspire, critique?"

• In 10-15 words, create a reminder question or statement you can use to quickly assess whether you are on course with your goal. Because I prefer Introversion, my reminder asks whether my calendar reflects meeting with others as well as time for my own creativity.

Sound simplistic? Most people find that this kind of focused document takes at least two hours to create. They then post it prominently—by their computer, on a mirror, or wherever they might regularly reflect on whether or not they are being intentional.

Figure C10 Sample Priority Checklist™

Intentional Leadership
My Priority Focus

Goal: **Increase influence in industry** **INFJ**

1. <u>**Relationships**</u> – Who might inspire, guide, critique?

> ➤ *Does my calendar reflect collaboration and networking as well as creativity and reflection?*

2. <u>**Expertise**</u> – Who can help me be politically savvy?

> ➤ *Who is my sounding board? Who tells me when I'm being an idiot?*

3. <u>**Creativity with the Known**</u> – Where should I dig deeper with what I've created?

> ➤ *How am I staying energized to develop, expand and promote the tools and ideas I believe can help others?*

Jane A. G. Kise, Ed.D., Principal
Differentiated Coaching Associates, LLC
<u>www.janekise.com</u>

<u>www.janekise.com</u>
© Differentiated Coaching Associates, LLC

Source: Map template copyright by Polarity Partnerships, LLC

For Further Reading on Polarity Thinking

Johnson, Barry. *Polarity Management: Identifying and Managing Unsolvable Problems.* Amherst, MA: HRD, 1992.

Kise, Jane A.G. *Unleashing the Positive Power of Differences: Polarity Thinking for Our Schools.* Thousand Oaks, CA: Corwin, 2014.

Seidler, Margaret. *Power Surge: A Conduit for Enlightened Leadership.* Amherst, MA: HRD, 2008.

To a parent who complained that teachers have it easy, an experienced educator replied, "You're right. It's just like hosting a birthday party. For 30 children who need to be engaged in successful learning experiences. Plus, you're the only adult, they stay all day, and then come back for another 179 parties." Daunting, isn't it? And, being a school leader is like hosting several such parties at once.

I spend a good portion of my time working with schools and find that the essential work of principals, superintendents, teacher leaders and other education leaders fits easily within the 12 Lenses of Leadership. However, there are some unique responsibilities and terms.

In a book I co-wrote with school principal Beth Russell, *Differentiated School Leadership*[4], we did an extensive review of research that revealed 26 separate essential roles and responsibilities for principals that foster student success. That same research also indicated that few individuals have the time, talents, or interests that would allow them to fill all 26 roles. Being intentional about using one's own strengths while attending somehow to related blind spots fosters the creation of strong leadership teams.

Matching Leadership Priorities and School Leadership Roles

School leaders will find that the 40 priorities listed on pages 168-9 are as integral to their work as other leaders find them. To gain insights into how your natural leadership style fits with the initiatives or practices you are being asked to implement,

1. Articulate, in a brief sentence of 6-8 words, one of your current goals. Instead of a general goal such as "Improve test scores" or "Lead implementation of new reading curriculum," aim for something such as "Improve student ability to explain mathematical thinking" or "Increase teacher comfort with new curriculum."

2. With that goal in mind, chose the ten priorities you believe are most essential for reaching that goal. The priorities are listed on pages 168-9. Or, use the Intentional Leadership Priority Cards.*

3. Once you've identified your top priorities, use Chart D to understand how your priorities match up with key roles for school leaders. Highlight the 10 you have chosen and then ask yourself several questions to ensure you've identified the right priorities.

    a. If I focus on the lenses indicated by my priorities, am I overlooking any lens (or school leadership role) that is vital to success?

    b. How do these relate to my personality type? Will accomplishing this goal be natural for me? A stretch? Do I need to partner with someone who enjoys a leadership role that is difficult for me? *Note that the matching of roles and personality type preferences only indicates a natural tendency for people with that preference to be more interested in those responsibilities. It does not indicate skill levels or individual interests.*

    c. Should I focus on my strengths or in this case will overusing my strengths lead to vulnerability in a key blind spot?

    d. Do I have a skill development need that has to become a priority focus?

---

* To order the Intentional Leadership Priority Cards, visit www.janekise.com

As described for all leaders in the "Polarity Thinking and Intentional Leadership" in Appendix, deciding whether to focus on strengths or blind spots depends on the situation. To decide, ask yourself, "If I don't focus on this Leadership Lenses in this situation, will I greatly increase my risk of somehow derailing?"

To become even more intentional about the goals and lenses you have chosen, create a priority checklist, as described on page 176. That checklist, and related action steps, can become a vital reference point for considering whether the school's goals truly align with time, resources, and the students and adults in the building!

The 12 Lenses of Leadership, Priorities, and School Leadership Roles

Type	Extraversion	Introversion
Lens 1	**Outer Focus**	**Inner Focus**
	Balancing action and reflection, engagement and solitude	
Priorities	*Networking, Relationships*	*Individuality, Personal Development*
Roles	**Being visible:** making systematic, frequent visits to classrooms; being highly visible to teachers, students, and parents	**Providing time for reflection:** guiding inquiry-based reflection on actions, interactions, goals, and possibilities
	Being situationally aware: understanding student/staff dynamics; noting potential issues and solutions	
	Gathering input: seeking staff involvement in setting priorities, goals; gathering input on important decisions	
Lens 2	**Breadth**	**Depth**
	Staying current on opportunities and developing expertise for lasting impact	
Priorities	*Variety, Influence*	*Depth, Legacy*
		Learning from positive and negative results: encouraging reflective practices to look beyond obvious cause/effect
Lens 3	**Leadership**	**Listening**
	Guide and develop others while helping them learn to guide themselves	
Priorities	*Mentoring, Promoting*	*Empowering, Connecting*
	Advocating for the school: reaching out to all stakeholders—staff, students, parents, community	**Delaying decisions to allow for reflection:** building in time to allow stakeholders to reflect before coming to closure

Type	Sensing	Intuition
Lens 4	**Reality**	**Vision**
	Manage the tension between what is and what might be in your situation	
Priorities	*Loyalty, Accountability*	*Visioning, Optimism*
	Maintaining school focus and evaluating strategy implementation: ensuring that resources are adequate to reach goals and chosen action steps are effective	**Setting school direction:** communicating strong ideals and beliefs that lead to student achievement
	Setting clear expectations and providing feedback: ensuring that staff understand their roles and responsibilities in implementing best practices	**Influencing beliefs:** transforming assumptions to change habits and affect practices
Lens 5	**The Known**	**The New**
	Manage the tension between building on current success and moving beyond it	
Priorities	*Experience, Creativity with the Known*	*Challenge, Creativity with the New*
	Managing school administrative processes: working with budgets, staffing, schedules, etc.	**Acting as change agent and optimizer:** challenging the status quo and inspiring others, leading new innovations
Lens 6	**Clarity**	**Ambiguity**
	Manage the tension between standardizing and remaining open to new processes and ideas	
Priorities	*Efficiency, Dependability*	*Openness, Originality*
	Establishing standard operating procedures and routines: identifying and embedding best practices in school culture	**Being open:** allowing diverse opinions and dissent and encouraging teachers to reach school goals in multiple ways

Type	Thinking	Feeling
Lens 7	**Logic**	**Values**
	Manage the tension between universal principles and individual truths	
Priorities	*Fair-Mindedness*	*Empathy*
		Incorporating qualitative data into decisions: using student and staff surveys, focus groups, parent input, etc.

Lens 8	Outcomes	People
	Move toward organizational success while building a dedicated, cohesive team	
Priorities	*Results*	*Harmony*
	Aligning curriculum and standards: guiding teachers to align what is taught with what students need to know	**Building relationships:** understanding the personal needs of teachers and the significant events in their lives
	Using data, assessment, and testing effectively: ensuring that assessment and other data is useful, timely, and informs instruction	
Lens 9	Individual Trust	Team Trust
	Honor individual strengths and initiative while building atmosphere and trust for collaboration	
Priorities	*Expertise, Autonomy*	*Appreciation, Collaboration*
	Gaining extensive knowledge of curriculum, instruction, and assessment: studying and providing information to staff on cutting-edge theory and practice	**Teambuilding:** leading for effective collaboration
	Being involved in instructional decisions: working with teachers on decisions about instruction, both content and processes	**Showing appreciation, recognizing accomplishments:** formalizing frequent, regular acknowledgement of successes

Type	Judging	Perceiving
Lens 10	Planning	Flexibility
	Set benchmarks and plans while responding to ever-changing environments	
Priorities	*Organization*	*Adaptability*
	Using "next action" thinking: identifying concrete steps to take once decisions are made	**Being flexible:** adapting one's leadership style to the needs of the situation
	Establishing goals and maintaining focus: consistently addressing the same goals throughout the school year	
Lens 11	Goal Orientation	Engagement
	Plan for the long haul while keeping joy in the moment	
Priorities	*Achievement, Perseverance*	*Enjoyment, Fulfillment*
Lens 12	Limits	Opportunities
	Create an environment where people can negotiate among work demands and other aspects of life	
Priorities	*Balance*	*Discovery*

Intentional Leadership Tools

Visit www.janekise.com for complete information

Intentional Leadership Certification

*Help your clients develop greater self-mastery and clearer focus
so they can become the leaders others want to follow*

Only a few leadership development efforts produce better leaders.
Why? They fail to account for context, are detached from the real
work of leadership, underestimate key biases, fail to measure results.
This program provides a toolkit that helps you and your clients avoid
all of these traps.

Intentional Leadership Coaching features

> **Proven tools** for self-awareness to help your client understand their strengths, how related
> blind spots might contribute to leadership derailment, and how their profile compares to
> other leaders
>
> > *Explore using the frameworks of psychological type (popularized through the MBTI®) and
> > emotional intelligence for coaching conversations around roles and priorities.*
> >
> > *Those not certified in these instruments will gain experience with ethical ways to use the
> > theories within the context of Intentional Leadership Coaching.*
>
> **A leadership framework** that encompasses 12 key leadership concerns to help clients under-
> stand which roles best fit their natural styles, which they tend to overlook, and which are
> most essential to reaching specific goals
>
> > *The 12 Lenses of Intentional Leadership were derived from research on essential leader-
> > ship tasks and describe 12 key tensions leaders face*
>
> **A focusing process leaders** can use again and again to choose the right priorities given who
> they are, who they are leading, their current realities, and where they need to go
>
> > *Guide clients through the Intentional Leadership process as, with a specific goal in mind,
> > they sift through priorities, the Leadership Lenses, and their own profile to develop a clear
> > plan for action*

*--Certified Coaches gain access to the online Intentional Leadership
Audit, Leadership Resource Library and Coaching Reports--*

Priority Cards

*This deck of 40 Priority Cards and 12 Leadership
Lens Cards deepens coaching conversations as clients
physically narrow down their priorities to gain focus
for their goals. $19.95. Details at www.janekise.com*

Notes

Chapter 1. Learning From Intentional—and Unintentional—Leaders

1. James M. Kouzes and Barry Z. Posner, *The Truth About Leadership: The No-Fads, Heart-of-the-Matter Facts You Need to Know* (San Francisco: Jossey-Bass, 2010), 1.

2. The MBTI is published by Consulting Psychologists Press, www.cpp.com.

3. The EQ-i 2.0 is published by Multi Health Systems, www.mhs.com.

4. Steven J. Stein and Howard E. Book, *The EQ Edge: Emotional Intelligence and Your Success*, rev. ed. (San Francisco: Jossey-Bass, 2006).

5. Cary Cherness et al. "Emotional Intelligence: What Does the Research Really Indicate," *Educational Psychologist* 41, no. 4 (2006): 239–45.

6. Ibid.

7. Marian Ruderman and Rueven Bar-On, "The Impact of Emotional Intelligence on Leadership," accessed February 24, 2012, http://downloads.mhs.com/ei/ID%23191_The%20Impact%20of%20EI%20on%20Leadership.pdf.

8. Tom Rath, *StrengthsFinder 2.0* (New York: Gallup Press, 2007).

9. Robert E. Kaplan, Wilfred Drath, and Joan R. Kofodimos, *High Hurdles: The Challenge of Executive Self-Development* (Greensborough, NC: Center for Creative Leadership, 1985).

10. Jim Collins, "Level 5 Leadership: The Triumph of Humility and Fierce Resolve," *Harvard Business Review* 83, no. 7/8 (2005): 136–46.

11. K. Anders Ericsson, Michael J. Prietula, and Edward T. Cokely, "The Making of an Expert," *Harvard Business Review* 85, no. 7/8 (2007): 118.

12. Jonathan Haidt, *The Happiness Hypothesis: Finding Modern Truth in Ancient Wisdom* (New York: Basic Books, 2006), 66.

13. Kathryn Schulz, *Being Wrong: Adventures in the Margin of Error* (New York: Ecco, 2010).

14. Jim Collins and Morten T. Hansen, *Great by Choice: Uncertainty, Chaos and Luck: Why Some Thrive Despite Them All* (New York: HarperCollins, 2011).

Chapter 2. A Framework for Strengths, Growth, and Those Pesky Pitfalls

1. Robert Ludlum, *The Janson Directive* (New York: St. Martin's Press, 2002), 176.

2. Jim Collins and Morten T. Hansen, *Great by Choice: Uncertainty, Chaos and Luck: Why Some Thrive Despite Them All* (New York: HarperCollins, 2011).

3. Sue G. Clancy, "STJs and Change: Resistance, Reaction, or Misunderstanding?" in *Developing Leaders: Research and Applications in Psychological Type and Leadership Development*, ed. Catherine Fitzgerald and Linda K. Kirby (Palo Alto, CA: Consulting Psychologists Press, 1997), 415–38.

4. My colleague Hile Rutledge of OKA (www.oka-online.com) shared this phrasing with me.

5. Isabel Briggs Myers et al., *MBTI Manual: A Guide to the Development and Use of the Myers-Briggs Type Indicator*, 3rd ed. (Palo Alto, CA: Consulting Psychologists Press, 1998), 3.

6. Nancy J. Barger and Linda K. Kirby, *The Challenge of Change in Organizations: Helping Employees Thrive in the New Frontier* (Palo Alto, CA: Consulting Psychologists Press, 1995).

Chapter 3. Balancing Outer and Inner Focus

1. Gareth Cook, "The Power of Introverts: A Manifesto for Quiet Brilliance," *Scientific American*, accessed February 24, 2012, www.scientificamerican.com/article.cfm?id=the-power-of-introverts&page=2.

2. Jeff Dyer, Hal Gregersen, and Clayton M. Christensen, *The Innovator's DNA: Mastering the Five Skills of Disruptive Innovators* (Cambridge, MA: Harvard Business Review Press, 2011), 113.

3. Steven J. Stein and Howard E. Book, *The EQ Edge: Emotional Intelligence and Your Success*, rev. ed. (San Francisco: Jossey-Bass, 2006), 102.

4. Marian Ruderman and Rueven Bar-On, "The Impact of Emotional Intelligence on Leadership," accessed February 24, 2012, http://downloads.mhs.com/ei/ID%23191_The%20Impact%20of%20EI%20on%20Leadership.pdf.

5. The MBTI Step II is published by CPP. In addition to the four preference scales reported in the Step I report, there are five subscales, or "facets," for

each of the preference pairs that describe different ways people use and express each of the preferences.

Chapter 4. Balancing Breadth and Depth

1. Daniel H. Pink, *Drive: The Surprising Truth About What Motivates Us* (New York: Riverhead, 2010).

2. Howard Book, "When Enhanced EI Is Associated with Leadership Derailment" in *Handbook for Developing Emotional and Social Intelligence: Best Practices, Case Studies, and Strategies,* ed. Marcia Hughes, Henry L. Thompson, and James Bradford Terrell (San Francisco: Pfeiffer, 2009), 73–95.

3. Jim Collins, *Good to Great: Why Some Companies Make the Leap and Others Don't* (New York: HarperCollins, 2001).

4. Isaiah Berlin, *The Hedgehog and the Fox: An Essay on Tolstoy's View of History* (New York: Touchstone, 1970).

Chapter 5. Balancing Leadership With Listening

1. W. Brad Johnson and Charles R. Ridley, *The Elements of Mentoring,* rev. ed., 2nd ed. (New York: Palgrave Macmillan, 2008), xi.

2. Janette Long, "The Dark Side of Mentoring" (Paper, AARE Conference, Newcastle, AU, 1994).

3. Ibid. chapter 2.

4. Brian Hansford, Lee Tennent, and Lisa Catherine Ehrich, "Business Mentoring: Help or Hindrance?" *Mentoring & Tutoring: Partnership in Learning* 10, no. 2 (2002): 101–15, accessed September 14, 2012, doi:10.1080/1361126022000002428.

5. Dario Nardi, *Neuroscience of Personality: Brain Savvy Insights for All Types of People* (Los Angeles: Radiance House, 2011).

6. Thomas G. Crane, *Coaching for Leadership: How the World's Greatest Coaches Help Leaders Learn,* ed. Marshall Goldsmith, Laurence Lyons, and Alyssa Freas (San Francisco: Jossey-Bass, 2000).

7. William W. George, *True North: Discovering Your Authentic Leadership* (San Francisco: Wiley, 2007), 43.

Chapter 6. Balancing Reality With Vision

1. James M. Kouzes and Barry Z. Posner, *The Truth About Leadership: The No-Fads, Heart-of-the-Matter Facts You Need to Know* (San Francisco: Jossey-Bass, 2010).

2. Jim Collins and Jerry I. Porras, *Built to Last: Successful Habits of Visionary Companies* (San Francisco: HarperBusiness, 1994).

3. Dee Hock, *Birth of the Chaordic Age* (San Francisco: Berrett-Koehler, 1999).

4. Kathryn Schulz, *Being Wrong: Adventures in the Margin of Error* (New York: Ecco, 2010).

Chapter 7. Balancing the Known With the New

1. Tom Rath, *StrengthsFinder 2.0* (New York: Gallup Press, 2007).

2. Jim Collins, *Good to Great: Why Some Companies Make the Leap ... and Others Don't* (New York: HarperCollins, 2001), 81.

3. Chip Heath and Dan Heath, *Switch: How to Change Things When Change Is Hard* (New York: Broadway Books, 2010).

4. Rath, *StrengthsFinder 2.0.*

5. Gordon MacKenzie, *Orbiting the Giant Hairball: A Corporate Fool's Guide to Surviving With Grace* (New York: Viking, 1996).

6. Heath and Heath, *Switch.*

Chapter 8. Balancing Clarity With Ambiguity

1. "Employee Has Endless Supply of Good Ideas," National Public Radio, accessed September 14, 2012, www.npr.org/templates/transcript/transcript.php?storyId=12430160.

2. Henry L. Thompson, *The Stress Effect: Why Smart Leaders Make Dumb Decisions—and What to Do About It* (San Francisco: Jossey-Bass, 2010). Chapter 7, "Developing Cognitive Resilience," is helpful in developing sound decision-making strategies under stress.

3. Daniel H. Pink, *Drive: The Surprising Truth About What Motivates Us* (New York: Riverhead, 2010).

4. Roger Pearman, *Introduction to Type and Emotional Intelligence: Pathways to Performance* (Mountain View, CA: Consulting Psychologists Press, 2002).

5. Margaret J. Wheatley, *Leadership and the New Science: Discovering Order in a Chaotic World*, 3rd ed. (San Francisco: Berrett-Kohler, 2006), 65.

6. Kees van der Heijden, *Scenarios: The Art of Strategic Conversation* (New York: Wiley, 1996), 119.

Chapter 9. Balancing Logic and Values

1. John Lehrer, *How We Decide* (New York: Houghton Mifflin Harcourt, 2009).

2. Dario Nardi, *Neuroscience of Personality: Brain Savvy Insights for All Types of People* (Los Angeles: Radiance House, 2011).

3. Daniel Goleman, Richard Boyatzis, and Annie McKee, *Primal Leadership: Realizing the Power of Emotional Intelligence* (Boston: Harvard Business School Press, 2002).

4. Steven J. Stein and Howard E. Book, *The EQ Edge: Emotional Intelligence and Your Success*, rev. ed. (San Francisco: Jossey-Bass, 2006), 134.

5. Rich Handley, "Advanced EQ-i Interpretation Techniques: The Concepts of Drag, Balance and Leverage," in *Handbook for Developing Emotional and Social Intelligence: Best Practices, Case Studies, and Strategies*, ed. Marcia Hughes, Henry L. Thompson, and James Bradford Terrell (San Francisco: Pfeiffer, 2009), 97–110.

6. Zachary Sheaffer et al., "Downsizing Strategies and Organizational Performance: A Longitudinal Study," *Management Decision* 47, no. 6 (2009): 950–74.

Chapter 10. Balancing Outcomes With People

1. Walter Isaacson, *Steve Jobs* (New York: Simon & Schuster, 2011).

2. Mike Hoban, "Knowing When to Embrace Leadership's 'Dark Side,'" *Fast Company*, accessed May 23, 2012, www.Fastcompany.com/1830247 /knowing-when-to-embrace-leaderships-dark-side?goback=%Egde_1345567 _member_115289983.

Chapter 11. Balancing Individual Trust With Team Trust

1. Tom DeMarco and Timothy Lister, *Peopleware: Productive Projects and Teams*, 2nd ed. (New York: Dorset House, 1999).

2. Mary H. McCaulley, "Predictions About Teams" (training handout, Gainesville, FL: Center for Applications of Psychological Type, n.d.).

3. Margaret J. Wheatley, *Leadership and the New Science: Discovering Order in a Chaotic World*, 3rd ed. (San Francisco: Berrett-Kohler, 2006), 40.

4. Steven Karau and Kipling Williams, "Social Loafing: A Meta-Analytic Review and Theoretical Integration," *Journal of Personality and Social Psychology* 65 (1993): 681–706.

5. Adrian Furnham, "The Brainstorming Myth," *Business Strategy Review* 11, no. 4 (2000): 21.

6. Patrick Lencioni, *Overcoming the Five Dysfunctions of a Team: A Field Guide for Leaders, Managers, and Facilitators* (San Francisco: Jossey-Bass, 2005),

Chapter 12. Balancing Planning With Flexibility

1. Barbara Tuchman, *The Guns of August* (New York: Ballantine, 1962).

2. "Dwight D. Eisenhower: Speech to National Defense Executive Reserve Conference on November 14," The American Presidency Project, accessed March 1, 2012, www.presidency.ucsb.edu/ws/index.php.

3. Henry Mintzberg, *The Rise and Fall of Strategic Planning: Reconceiving Roles for Planning, Plans, Planners* (New York: Free Press, 1993).

4. Alan Fine with Rebecca R. Merrill, *You Already Know How to Be Great: A Simple Way to Remove Interference and Unlock Your Greatest Potential* (New York: Portfolio Penguin, 2010).

5. Abraham Sagie, "Leader Direction and Employee Participation in Decision Making: Contradictory or Compatible Practices?" *Applied Psychology: An International Review* 46 (1997), 387–415.

Chapter 13. Balancing Goal Orientation With Engagement

1. Andrea Hershatter and Molly Epstein, "Millennials and the World of Work: An Organization and Management Perspective," *Journal of Business & Psychology* 25, no. 2 (2010): 211–223, accessed September 14, 2012, doi:10.1007/s10869-010-9160-y.

2. "Millennials at Work: Perspectives From a New Generation," PriceWaterhouseCoopers, accessed July 17, 2009, www.pwc.com/gx/en /forms/gxengallsmillennialsatworkperspectivesfromanewgeneration.jhtml.

3. Brenda Kowske, Rena Rasch, and Jack Wiley, "Millennials' (Lack of) Attitude Problem: An Empirical Examination of Generational Effects on Work Attitudes," *Journal of Business & Psychology* 25, no. 2 (2010): 265–79, accessed September 14, 2012, doi:10.1007/s10869-010-9171-8.

4. Karen Myers and Kamyab Sadaghiani, "Millennials in the Workplace: A Communication Perspective on Millennials' Organizational Relationships and Performance," *Journal of Business & Psychology* 25, no. 2 (2010): 225–38, accessed September 14, 2012, doi:10.1007/s10869-010-9172-7.

5. Jim Collins and Morten T. Hansen, *Great by Choice: Uncertainty, Chaos and Luck: Why Some Thrive Despite Them All* (New York: HarperCollins, 2011).

6. Po Bronson, *What Should I Do With My Life? The True Story of People Who Answered the Ultimate Question* (New York: Random House, 2002), 119.

7. Scott Flander, "Millennial Magnets," *Human Resources Executive Online*, accessed February 18, 2012, www.hreonline.com/HRE/story.jsp?storyId =84159035.

Chapter 14. Balancing Limits With Opportunities

1. Tony Schwartz, Jean Gomes, and Catherine McCarthy, *The Way We're Working Isn't Working: The Four Forgotten Needs That Energize Great Performance* (New York: Free Press, 2010).

2. Mark R. Rosekind et al., "The Cost of Poor Sleep: Workplace Productivity Loss and Associated Costs," *Journal of Occupational and Environmental Medicine*, 52, no. 1 (2012): 91–98.

3. Nanci Hellmich, "What Ails Us: 'Sitting Disease,'" *USA Today*, accessed February 29, 2012, www.usatoday.com/printedition/life/20090122 /fidgetfactor22_st.art.htm.

4. Schwartz, Gomes, and McCarthy, *The Way We're Working Isn't Working.*

5. Gordon D. Lawrence, *Finding the Zone: A Whole New Way to Maximize Mental Potential* (New York: Prometheus, 2010), 118.

Epilogue: Intentional Success

1. Po Bronson, *What Should I Do With My Life? The True Story of People Who Answered the Ultimate Question* (New York: Random House, 2002), 119.

Appendix

1. Gordon, Lawrence. *Descriptions of the 16 Types* (Gainesville, FL: Center for Applications of Psychological Type, 1998).

2. Dario, Nardi. *Neuroscience of Personality: Brain Savvy Insights for All Types of People* (Los Angeles: Radiance House, 2011).

3. Johnson, Barry. *The Polarity Approach to Continuity and Transformation* (Sacramento, CA: Polarity Partnerships, LLC, 2012), 4.

4. Kise, Jane A. G. and Beth Russel. *Differentiated School Leadership: Effective Collaboration, Communication, and Change Through Personality Type* (Thousand Oaks, CA: Corwin, 2008).

Index

About the Author

Jane A. G. Kise, EdD, is a consultant with extensive experience in teambuilding, conflict resolution, and executive coaching. Her other areas of expertise include strategic planning and education consulting. She has worked with Minneapolis Public Schools, the Bush Foundation, Twin Cities Public Television, ConAgra, and other large and small businesses, as well as with numerous education and community banking organizations. In addition to having an active client base in North America, Kise has keynoted and conducted workshops in several European countries, Saudi Arabia, New Zealand, and Australia.

In 2005, Kise received the Isabel Briggs Myers Award for her research on differentiated coaching. In 2007, she received the Journal of Psychological Type Award for Best Application of Psychological Type for her research on coaching teachers for change. In 2011 she received the Gordon Lawrence Educational Achievement Award.

She is author or coauthor of more than twenty books, including *Differentiated Coaching, Creating a Coaching Culture for Professional Learning Communities, Work It Out: Using Personality Type to Improve Team Performance, Using the MBTI® Tool in Organizations,* and *Introduction to Type and Coaching.* In addition, Kise's articles have appeared in *Educational Leadership, The Bulletin of Psychological Type, Guideposts, Writer's Digest,* and many other magazines.

Kise is a master practitioner of the Myers-Briggs Type Indicator®, the EQ-i, and the Strong Interest Inventory® and frequently speaks or consults using these instruments. Her research and writing on coaching involve integrating the theories behind these tools to differentiate coaching practices and inform 360 assessments and other leadership development practices.

She is past president of the Association for Psychological Type International, the Minnesota Chapter of National League of American Pen Women, and a faculty member of the Center for Applications of Psychological Type. She is a member of several honor societies, including Phi Beta Kappa. She previously worked as an examiner for the Federal Reserve Bank of Minneapolis and as a financial analyst for Norwest Corporation.

Books from Allworth Press

Allworth Press is an imprint of Skyhorse Publishing, Inc. Selected titles are listed below.

The Art of Digital Branding, Revised Edition
by Ian Cocoran (6 x 9, 272 pages, paperback, $19.95)

Brand Thinking and Other Noble Pursuits
by Debbie Millman (6 x 9, 320 pages, paperback, $19.95)

Career Solutions for Creative People
by Dr. Ronda Ormont (6 x 9, 320 pages, paperback, $27.50)

Corporate Creativity: Developing an Innovative Organization
by Thomas Lockwood and Thomas Walton (6 x 9, 256 pages, paperback, $24.95)

Effective Leadership for Nonprofit Organizations
by Thomas Wolf (6 x 9, 192 pages, paperback, $16.95)

Emotional Branding, Revised Edition
by Marc Gobe (6 x 9, 344 pages, paperback, $19.95)

From Idea to Exit: The Entrepreneurial Journey
by Jeffrey Weber (6 x 9, 272 pages, paperback, $19.95)

Infectious: How to Connect Deeply and Unleash the Energetic Leader Within
by Achim Nowak (6 x 9, 256 pages, paperback, $19.95)

Millennial Rules: How to Sell, Serve, Surprise & Stand Out in a Digital World
by T. Scott Gross (6 x 9, 208 pages, paperback, $16.95)

Peak Performance Under Pressure
by Bill Driscoll (6 x 9, 224 pages, paperback, $19.95)

The Pocket Small Business Owner's Guide to Building Your Business
by Kevin Devine (5 ¼ x 8 ¼, 256 pages, paperback, $14.95)

The Pocket Small Business Owner's Guide to Business Plans
by Brian Hill and Dee Power (5 ½ x 8 ¼, 224 pages, paperback, $14.95)

The Pocket Small Business Owner's Guide to Negotiating
by Kevin Devine (5 ½ x 8 ¼, 224 pages, paperback, $14.95)

Rebuilding the Brand: How Harley-Davidson Became King of the Road
by Clyde Fessler (6 x 9, 128 pages, paperback, $14.95)

To see our complete catalog or to order online, please visit *www.allworth.com*.

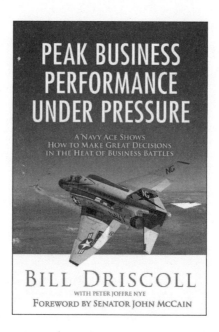

Peak Business Performance Under Pressure
A Navy Ace Shows How to Make Great Decisions in the Heat of Business Battles

by Bill Driscoll with Peter Joffre Nye

Foreword by Senator John McCain

In enemy airspace, high above the treetops of North Vietnam, two US F-4 Phantom jet fighters have downed their fifth enemy plane, thus securing their new status as "Aces." The skies are finally quiet, and the safety of the ocean is just ahead. But in that brief moment of victory, they are blindsided by a surface-to-air missile.

Bill "Willy" Driscoll, one of the most highly decorated Naval Flight Officers of the last fifty years, demonstrates how his TOPGUN training prepared him for both life-or-death aerial dogfights and the demands of difficult business decisions. His remarkable military experiences, his twenty-six-year award-winning career in the highly competitive Southern California commercial real estate market, and personal interviews with twenty-six other Ace pilots and over two-hundred business executives serve as a blueprint for achieving extraordinary results under the most difficult circumstances organizations face each day.

Topics include preparation, risk assessment, team building, focus and listening, self-evaluation and improvement, avoiding pitfalls, and much more.

$19.95 Paperback • ISBN 978-1-62153-424-2

From Idea to Exit
The Entrepreneurial Journey

by Jeffrey Weber

This book is a call to action if you have any of the following Symptoms of Entrepreneurial Envy: incurable idea generation; difficulty taking action on your ideas; fear, preventing you from pursuing your dreams; a strong desire to be your own boss.

From Idea to Exit: The Entrepreneurial Journey addresses the mystery, fear, and risk of starting, running, and selling a business. By following the entertaining and informative true story of Jeffrey Weber, you'll learn his proven methodologies for entrepreneurial success. Jeffrey Weber's story is extraordinary and he outlines a successful entrepreneurial journey through four phases: idea, startup, running, and exit.

While most small business books cover niche components of the start-up model, *From Idea to Exit* takes a more comprehensive approach, tackling the entire entrepreneurial journey from the initial seed idea through a well-planned exit strategy. Through a persuasive narrative, the author draws from his own success a practical call to action for those who dream of taking that first big step.

$19.95 Paperback • ISBN 978-1-62153-427-3

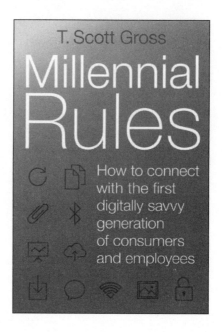

Millennial Rules

How to Connect with the First Digitally Savvy Generation of Consumers and Employees

by T. Scott Gross

In today's digital world, the Baby Boomers and Generation X are giving way to a new generation of consumers: the Millennials. These tech-savvy consumers—bearing the mantra "my way, right away, why pay?"—want quick, customizable service that is negotiated on their terms and delivers great value. And when Millennials want help, they want it now; when they don't want help, they expect the sales staff to be invisible.

In *Millennial Rules: How to Connect with the First Digitally Savvy Generation of Consumers and Employees*, veteran business owner T. Scott Gross demystifies the newest generation and shares how businesses can meet and exceed Millennials' expectations to make the sale—without resorting to tricks and gimmicks. Invisible selling is built on ethical, common-sense business practices that yield success across the board, regardless of niche or industry. Armed with research into generational consumer preferences, humor, and a wealth of experience, Gross tackles the looming question, "How can you disappear and still deliver quality service?" The answer, he suggests, is by emphasizing serving above selling, a strategy that will make organizations successful not just with Millennials, but with all generations.

$16.95 Paperback • ISBN 978-1-62153-423-5

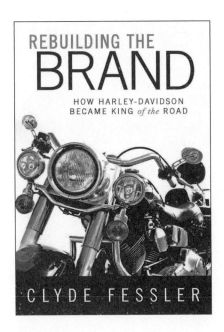

Rebuilding the Brand
How Harley-Davidson Became King of the Road

by Clyde Fessler

In the early 1980s, Harley-Davidson was on the verge of bankruptcy. In the general public's opinion, quality was substandard—both of motorcycles and riders. Harleys leaked oil and often broke down. Riders were roughnecks, out to raise hell. The Harley-Davidson brand was tarnished. What's more, the charges were true.

By the mid-1980s, Harley couldn't produce enough bikes to keep the public happy. Dealers were selling bikes off the showroom floor, struggling to assuage customers frustration. And today, Harley-Davidson is a model brand. Harley-Davidson isn't just a motorcycle company anymore. It is a community, a look, a source of self-expression, an all-American appeal for freedom—all expressed in one little logo.

Rebuilding the Brand: How Harley-Davidson Became King of the Road is the story of how a core group led a team of not only marketing folks but also employees, management, dealers, and vendors to rebuild the Harley-Davidson image. Told through the perspective of Clyde Fessler—who held several positions within Harley, from head of marketing services to VP of business development—*Rebuilding the Brand* provides dynamic branding information couched in an entertaining story.

$14.95 Paperback • ISBN 978-1-62153-425-9

Brand Thinking and Other Noble Pursuits

by Debbie Millman

Foreword by Rob Walker

We are now living in a world with over one hundred brands of bottled water. The United States alone is home to over 45,000 shopping malls. And there are more than nineteen million customized beverage choices a barista can whip up at your local Starbucks. Whether it's good or bad, the real question is why we behave this way in the first place. Why do we telegraph our affiliations or our beliefs with symbols, signs, and codes?

Brand Thinking and Other Noble Pursuits contains twenty interviews with the world's leading designers and thinkers in branding. The interviews contain spirited views on how and why humans have branded the world around us, and the ideas, inventions, and insight inherent in the search.

$19.95 Paperback • ISBN 978-1-62153-247-7

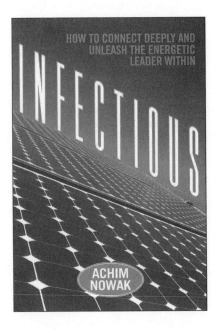

Infectious
How to Connect Deeply and Unleash the Energetic Leader Within

by Achim Nowak

Technology has transformed the way we communicate. We send and receive more and more emails every day. We text. We tweet. We have reduced our communications down to efficient sound bites—and at the same time, many of us seem to know less and less about how to connect. Deeply, profoundly connect.

In *Infectious*, acclaimed performance coach Achim Nowak introduces the reader to his powerful four Levels of Connection. Tested and honed through fifteen years of coaching senior-level executives around the globe, Nowak's techniques instantly transform the skills taught in traditional business communication and NLP programs. People who connect deeply with others connect on four levels; they shape conversations with effortless grace, and they play consciously with the unspoken elements of a connection—personal power, intention, and energy. The result? Infectious connections that accelerate personal success!

Infectious offers simple language cues that deepen and shift the art of conversation. It breaks the idea of power into five tangible plugs that we can turn to—and turn on. These plugs recharge the quality of our connection with anyone we meet. It shows how we can clarify our intentions, and how this clarification immediately fosters a more potent connection.

$19.95 Paperback • ISBN 978-1-62153-288-0

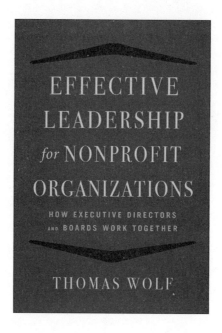

Effective Leadership for Nonprofit Organizations
How Executive Directors and Boards Work Together

by Thomas Wolf

Managing a nonprofit organization has many challenges. One key to success is building a strong relationship between the executive director and the board of trustees. This book is a treasure trove of information for navigating the personal, political, and legal minefields that cause so many nonprofits to fail. Dozens of case studies illuminate the key issues that often impede the progress of nonprofit organizations. Each chapter also contains a set of questions that enable leaders to reflect on the health of their own organization and also evaluate other nonprofits, as well as to create sustainable, effective business practices and productive working relationships. Topics discussed here include:

• Communication between managerial parties • Sharing powers and responsibilities • Fund-raising • Financial oversight and boundaries • Planning programs • Hiring and firing • Developing partnerships •Assessing business practices • Building productive working relationships • And much more

Whether you are an executive director, a board member, or someone contemplating either important role, *Effective Leadership for Nonprofit Organizations* is an excellent resource for understanding the dynamics of nonprofits and creating a strong organization.

$16.95 Paperback • ISBN 978-1-62153-287-3